D1260670

ITALIAN ARCHITECTURE UP TO 1750

Coloured tip-in plate to be pasted here

SIENA. *Palazzo Pubblico and Mangia Tower*

ITALIAN ARCHITECTURE
UP TO 1750

F. M. GODFREY
PH.D.

NEW YORK   **TAPLINGER PUBLISHING CO. INC.**   1971

FIRST AMERICAN EDITION PUBLISHED BY

TAPLINGER PUBLISHING CO. INC. 1971

200 PARK AVENUE SOUTH, NEW YORK NY 10003

LIBRARY OF CONGRESS CATALOGUE CARD NUMBER: 75-137662

(C) 1971 COPYRIGHT ALEC TIRANTI LTD., LONDON

MADE AND PRINTED IN GREAT BRITAIN

ISBN 0-8008-4270-7

CONTENTS

v

ACKNOWLEDGEMENTS

The author wishes to acknowledge his indebtedness to the scholarly works listed in the Bibliography and more especially to the volumes in the Pelican History of Art by K. J. Conant, R. Krautheimer, J. White and R. Wittkower; also to N. Pevsner's *Outlines* and *Dictionary*, to H. Decker's *Romanesque* and P. Murray's *Renaissance Architecture*.

F.G.M.

PHOTOGRAPHIC ACKNOWLEDGEMENTS

We wish to express our appreciation of the generous and willing help given us by the Director of the Italian State Tourist Office of London; also to the various authorities mentioned under the respective illustrations.

The Publishers

INTRODUCTION

A SURVEY of the visual arts of any period or country would not be complete without its architecture. The traditional division into styles is based upon architecture. Whoever speaks of Italian Gothic does not primarily think of Simone Martini or of the frescoes in the Campo Santo, but of the cathedrals in Siena and Orvieto. It has been claimed that architecture embraces all two- and three-dimensional arts, that its function is spatial as well as sculptural and pictorial. Architectural space is real, not illusionist. It is enclosed, shaped, imprisoned between walls, transformed into a habitat. Architecture is composed of man-made spatial entities where structural form, a material purpose and decorative qualities combine.

It is concerned with modelling volume and geometrical bodies, with voids and solids and, like painting, it relies on the effects of light and shadow, on colour contrasts, proportions and design. Moreover, the spiritual forces governing a given period condition its style. For ' a style in art ' wrote Nikolaus Pevsner ' belongs to the world of mind not of matter '.

This elusive quality, ' the spirit of the age ', shapes all architecture worthy of the name. This applies to the striking geometry and solidity of the Romanesque, the transcendental mystique of the Gothic, the measured harmony of the Renaissance or the dramatic complexity of the Baroque. Though architecture has no narrative content or iconography like the figurative arts, it nonetheless reflects a state of mind from tranquility to emotional exaltation.

Apart from the evolution of styles it is the inventiveness of individual artists, their genius for experiment, variation and discovery which most engage our attention. For it appears that in all great periods of architecture —though the basic forms of ecclesiastic and secular buildings assure a measure of continuity—the creative artists were allowed great freedom for their imaginative faculties.

Churches may be determined by the need to house large congregations and to reserve a zone for altar and clergy; but within the bounds of a cruciform or central plan or a combination of the two, a great variety of spatial and decorative solutions accrued; from the planar façades of the Romanesque, with or without arcading, to the sculptural articulations of the Gothic, the staid serenity and formal purity of the Early Renaissance to the massive grandiloquence of High Renaissance and Baroque.

In palace architecture the varying size and relationship of storeys and windows, the rough cyclopic stones used at ground floor level in contrast to the smooth masonry above, the vertical divisions by pilasters, the horizontals stressed by moulded cornices, the fanciful window surrounds and pediments and, above all, the arcaded courtyards within, nobly proportioned or extravagantly Mannerist, left great scope to the designing architect. The mosque-like domes in southern Italy, the Gothic tracery of Venetian palaces, the astounding cylindrical fortresses by Francesco di Giorgio, prismatic towers or embattled town halls, give some idea of the inventive variety in Italian architecture. Nor is it surprising that a Mediterranean country within the classical tradition should favour sculptural forms. Many of her greatest architects were primarily sculptors, from Giovanni Pisano and Arnolfo di Cambio to Michelangelo and Bernini. Leonardo did not build, but his architectural drawings influenced Bramante whose High Renaissance forms are reflected in Raphael's paintings. The impact of Piero della Francesca upon the superb Palace of Urbino becomes credible from the architectural ambience in his pictures.

The splitting of the arts into separate compartments was alien to Renaissance workshops. Men strove to become fully stretched individuals for which the Italians coined the term of *uomo universale*.

In his magisterial exposition *The Classical Language of Architecture* Sir John Summerson has laid bare the skeleton or ' grammar ' of Antique building practice and its continuity in all western architecture of the Renaissance, Mannerism, Baroque and Neo-Classicism, even to the threshold of our own age. Whether functional or decorative, the ' Orders ' play a vital part in the overall aspect of a building, determining its divisions and its scale. They are a set variety of columnar forms, Doric, Ionic and Corinthian, Tuscan and Composite, a fundamental module which the Ancients invented, Vitruvius systematized at the time of Augustus and to which Renaissance theorists from Alberti to Palladio adhered closely. Deriving from the colonnade of the temple, the Orders consist of the column with its base and capital and the connecting horizontal beams or entablature above: architrave, frieze and projecting cornice. The column takes its measure from the human figure, conveying masculine strength (Doric) or feminine grace (Ionic). But though the Orders condition the rhythm and proportion of façades, domes, courtyards, their weight-bearing function is limited and they admit of a great variety of shapes and size. Columns can be attached to heavy piers, incorporated into walls or flattened out into pilasters. They determine the spatial intervals of a building, especially when supporting arches, dividing window bays or scanning the storeys by a superimposed Order. Thus the Orders do not constitute a building, but they are the criteria of its harmony and proportion.

Monuments like the Roman Colosseum, the vaulted Basilica of Maxentius, the Triumphal arch of Constantine or the hemispherical dome of the Pantheon were the ineluctable examples for Renaissance architects and painters. The triple rows of arches and immured columns of the Colosseum, topped by a blind storey is such a primary source. Alberti and Mantegna, Bramante, Raphael and Michelangelo were imbued with the imposing architectural shapes of Imperial Rome; be it Masaccio's *trompe-l'oeil* behind his heroic Trinity in S. Maria Novella, the triumphal arch motif of Alberti's Tempio Malatestiano at Rimini and of S. Andrea (Mantua) or Mantegna's Eremitani frescoes at Padua, the grandiose coffered vaults in Raphael's *School of Athens* or again the sequence of triumphal arches in the nave-chapels of S. Peter's and of Il Gesù. Bramante's small temple in the cloister of S. Pietro in Montorio, akin to the Roman temple of Vesta, was considered the supreme achievement of the High Renaissance on a par with the monuments of Antiquity.

Bramante and the later churches of Brunelleschi revived classical architecture by creating new buildings in the spirit of the old. Michelangelo subjected classical forms, the canonical rules of Vitruvius to his sovereign imagination and freedom from convention. In his Medici Chapel and Library at S. Lorenzo (Florence), the functional becomes decorative. Blind windows and doors, combined into one ornamental whole, break up the wall surface; sculptural mouldings of exquisite design surround flat niches of aedicules; columns and pilasters are sunk into the walls with a supreme disregard of structural purpose. A staircase tossing down to the floor in curves is the *pièce de résistance* of the Laurentian Library. In his seventies, Michelangelo, turned architect, invented the giant Order of Corinthian pilasters, two storeys high, in the palaces of the Capitol and larger still in the apses of S. Peter's. In all media he transcended the rules and the norm, imposing his genius for sculptural articulation and invention. His influence on contemporaries and followers was incalculable, from Sangallo the Younger to Sansovino, Sanmicheli, Palladio, and ultimately to the giants of the Roman Baroque Bernini and Borromini.

Thus there was more than one Renaissance in Italy. Even small cities like Mantua (Giulio Romano) and Vicenza (Palladio) had their own. Giulio's Palazzo del Tè is remarkable as a Mannerist revolt against classical tyranny. He still uses the Orders, but built his walls of rough quarry stones, arches of wedge shaped quoins, columns smooth or twisted composing a long, low palace façade. His style is a titanic and emotive variant from the classical tradition. Palladio's on the other hand

3

was a learned and accurate revival of the Latin language of architecture, as in the two Orders of open colonnades in Palazzo Chiericati or the sculptural articulation of bays in his Venetian churches. Here half-columns attached to piers enframe arches and support a continuous entablature. A hundred years later, Bernini's Doric colonnade embracing S. Peter's square, has been called ' probably the most imposing assembly of columns in the world '. Built from 1656 onwards it demonstrates the suggestive force of Antiquity even at the height of the Roman Baroque. This grandiloquent array of columns, standing four deep and supporting a straight entablature is the swansong of classical art on Italian soil.

from Letarouilly

The Christian basilica had a vast nave, lit by large clerestorey windows, and divided from the lower aisles by colonnades. A rounded or rectangular apse with a raised platform was reserved for the ritual, the altar-canopy, bishop's throne and officiating clergy. This sanctuary was cut off from the lay-congregation not by columns but by railings and a triumphal arch. A separate entrance zone or narthex corresponded to the presbytery, and here (or in the aisles) the new converts who were not yet admitted to Mass, watched the service. Finally an outer court or atrium received the ' non-believers or postulants '. The spiritual centre of the Christian basilica was the shrine of saint or martyr as in S. Peter's which was built over the tomb of the first Apostle on a large site levelled out of the Vatican hill; or S. Paul's outside the City Walls. S. Sebastiano and S. Agnese were also tomb churches erected over underground martyria.

These great basilicas were cemetery churches or mausolea sheltering not only the protagonists of the faith but also many tombs of the Roman aristocracy who desired burial near the sacred shrines. The great size of the basilicas was due to their function as funerary banqueting halls and also to their need to accommodate vast crowds of pilgrims.

When Christianity and the influential hierarchy of its priesthood recommended itself to Constantine's *raison d'état*, he assigned to the bishop of Rome a vast imperial palace, the Lateran, and then proceeded to build the church of S. Giovanni in Laterano (320), consisting of a huge nave, four aisles and an apse, which became the cathedral of Rome. The pagan basilica in its Christian form was ' a new creation within an accustomed framework '. Even the triumphal arch of the Caesars became the solemn frame or entrance to the sanctuary, terminating the nave, a heroic surround for the Christian mysteries enacted there. Such were the premises underlying ecclesiastical architecture since the days of Constantine.

The arcaded forecourt of the basilica—nucleus of the monastic cloister—led to a covered portico attached to the lower part of the façade. The long nave and aisles were separated by four rows of columns supporting arches or straight entablatures, sometimes followed by a transept, a spatial interval between nave and apse. But the original Lateran basilica had no transept. In old S. Peter's on the other hand, nave and aisles were cut off by a spacious transverse unit. Only the apse was vaulted and flanked by two smaller rooms for the robing of the priests and the keeping of the sacraments. Domed and vaulted churches, designed on a central plan, were of Byzantine provenance and infrequent in Rome.

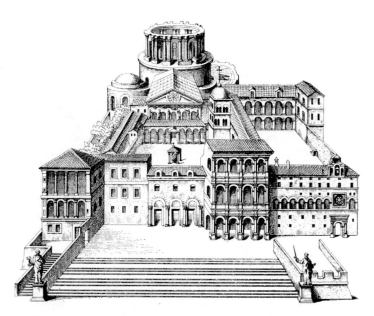

1. ROME. *Old S. Peter's with old pontifical palace on right and beginnings of new S. Peter's in background (from Letarouilly)*

1 Old S. Peter's was begun about 333 during Constantine's lifetime and imitated by Theodosius half a century later as a Martyrium of the

2 Apostle Paul. The essential feature of S. Peter's basilica was its ' continuous transept ' as high as the nave and projecting beyond the lines of the aisles. Together with the large apse it formed a separate church, screened off from the basilica by rows of columns. It was here that the shrine of the Apostle stood under a baldacchino raised on spiral columns. The great size of the transept was required for the worshippers at the Apostle's tomb and also for the clergy ministering at commemoration services. The place of the altar was probably near the triumphal arch, to give access to the communicants. But the apse was reserved for bishops and priests. The pilgrim approaching from the River Tiber entered the atrium through one of the three gates and passed the canopied fountain before reaching the monumental basilica with its four rows of twenty-two antique columns of polychrome marble and composite capitals, supporting a straight entablature. But the aisles were separated by arcades. These lay steeped in darkness, whereas nave and transept were flooded by light. The foundations of S. Peter's ran in an east-west direction according to the slope of the hill, so that the entrance portico was in the east, the sanctuary in the west. Moreover, the interior consisted of two almost separate parts,

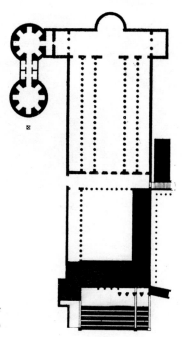

2. ROME. *Plan of Old S. Peter's*
(*reconstruction by Letarouilly*)

the martyrium incorporated in the transept and the congregational nave
and aisles. Their different purpose was expressed both 'functionally
and architecturally'.

Basically the three Christian basilicas that Constantine built over the
sacred sites such as that of the Nativity and of the Holy Sepulchre in
Jerusalem and the Tomb of the Apostle Peter in Rome, combined three
spatials units into one, along the longitudinal axis: atrium, aisles and apse.
But there were many variations of the basic scheme, relating mainly to
the number of aisles, the form of lighting, the existence, size and projection
of a transept, the shape of the apse. Some early churches had no transverse unit or no forecourt.

S. Paul's outside the City Walls, ordered by the Eastern Emperor **3**
Theodosius in 386, was faithfully rebuilt after the great fire of 1823 had
all but destroyed it. Yet though lacking the charism of an ancient place
of worship, it presents a true picture of the metropolitan scale and imperial
splendour which distinguished the two basilicas of the Apostle princes.
The total length, breadth and height are only a little less than those of Old
S. Peter's which it clearly imitates, especially in the continuous transept
and detached nave. An unbroken colonnade leads towards the triumphal
arch, the raised transept and single apse. These majestic granite columns

9

3. ROME. *Basilica of S. Paolo fuori le Mura*

support arches, not an entablature as in S. Peter's. Above them is a continuous cornice and a large expanse of wall, decorated with a row of medallions with busts of popes, and above them large windows alternating with painted panels and separated by pilasters. Fifth century mosaics decorate the triumphal arch, but those in the apse are of the thirteenth century.

The transept, as wide as the nave, projects only slightly and the width of the nave equals that of each pair of aisles, in harmony with the revival of classical proportions. The relentless progression of columns, lining the broad nave under the heavily gilded roof, is towards the arcaded transept, flooded by light from twelve windows and oculi. Here the relics of the Apostle are enshrined beneath a canopy designed and sculpted by Arnolfo di Cambio. S. Paolo fuori le Mura is only a modern replica of one of the oldest basilicas in Rome. Its marble columns disintegrated in the fire, its ceiling collapsed, its mosaics were damaged.

But plan and dimensions have been preserved by the meticulous restorer and allow us to visualize its original form. The magnificent cloister by Vassaletto of about 1330 with twisted, inlaid or fluted columns survives and also the ciborium over the altar and tomb of the Apostle. The altar is now in the east. There is no narthex, only a spacious modern atrium. But some of the finest basilicas, rotundas, and baptisteries of the greatest period (fourth to sixth century) have been impeccably preserved in Rome and Ravenna, and the impression is gained that with the forms and proportions of Antiquity something of its human dignity and repose was imparted to the Christian temple, together with the hieratic spirit of Byzantine mosaics.

82

10

4. ROME. *Basilica of S. Lorenzo fuori le Mura (photo: E.N.I.T. Rome)*

A remarkable basilica outside Rome, built between 432 and 578 to commemorate a martyred saint is S. Lorenzo fuori le Mura. It consists **4** of two churches telescoped into one. The sanctuary at the east was ' scooped ' out of a hill at a higher level than the nave from which it is reached by steps. The east end has galleried aisles to equate the height of the nave and to accommodate more worshippers at the shrine. The arched galleries with fluted columns and Corinthian capitals and the richly carved frieze of the presbytery are in strong contrast to the continuous cornice and trabeation over long rows of smooth Ionic columns in the nave. The two disparate halves of the vast basilica, built over a covered cemetery and the catacomb of the Saint, are only loosely joined, differing in level, style and structure, with the sanctuary serving as the spiritual and decorative climax.

A Renaissance of late Roman classical forms occurs during the fifth century under Pope Sixtus III, as the eurhythmic beauty of S. Maria **5** Maggiore (432-40) testifies. It is also the first basilica dedicated to the **260** Virgin Mary whom the Council of Ephesus had proclaimed the Mother of Christ. A wide nave is flanked by long rows of sturdy columns with Ionian capitals supporting a classic entablature. These are continued in the upper storey by pilasters enframing windows and painted panels. A precious mosaic frieze beneath the projecting cornice and the broad coffered ceiling enhance the perspective towards triumphal arch and rounded apse. Eight clerestorey windows shed light into the majestic

5. ROME Basilica of S. Maria Maggiore. Interior (photo : E.N.I.T. Rome)

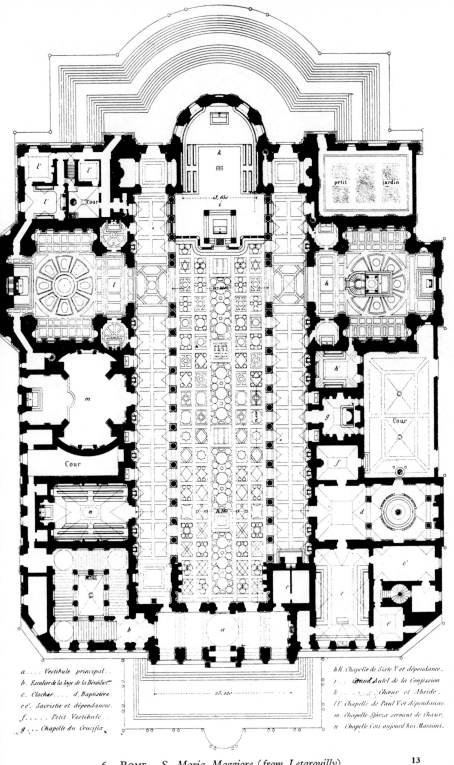

petit jardin

Cour

Cour

a.... Vestibule principal..
b. Escalier de la loge de la Bénédict.
c. Clocher.... d. Baptistère.
cc'. Sacristie et dépendances.
f..... Petit Vestibule...
g... Chapelle du Crucifix.

hh'. Chapelle de Sixte V et dépendance.
i.... Grand Autel de la Confession
k.... Chœur et Abside.
ll'. Chapelle de Paul V et dépendances.
m. Chapelle Sforza servant de Chœur.
n. Chapelle Cesi aujourd'hui Massimi.

7. ROME. *S. Sabina*

nave which follows classical laws of proportion where height equals
width. The rhythmic progression of the columns depends from their
6 diameter, their spacing and their number. As in antique temples they
bear the weight of the architraves directly without intervening arches,
and by their measured relation to nave-walls and aisles they hold the
regal interior in perfect equipoise.

7 Another impeccable but quite different example of the classical
revival is S. Sabina (422-33), the most perfect in shape and decoration.
The twenty-four fluted columns with Corinthian capitals of acanthus
leaves are of exceptional elegance, their gently swelling shafts like a musical
crescendo. These columns do not bear the weight of a continuous
entablature as in S. Maria Maggiore, but slender arches with marble
inlay of abstract design in spandrels, frieze and soffits. Large round
clerestorey windows correspond with the arches. The long narrow
aisles of S. Sabina are dark in contrast to the lofty, light-flooded nave

8. ROME. *S. Costanza*

which moves swiftly between graceful arcades towards the apse which is pierced by three windows. Planar wall surfaces blend with the polished marble inlay, and the interior is all harmony and serenity resulting from classical measure and proportion. S. Sabina expresses an Attic balance and dignity rather than the Christian aspirations to the otherworldly.

Early Christian basilicas are oriented towards the spiritual centre of the sanctuary by their long nave and arcades. But for martyria or mausolea, built over the shrine of saints, round structures evolved like S. Costanza and S. Stefano Rotondo; and polygonal ones for baptisteries like that of the Lateran in Rome or the Orthodox Baptistery in Ravenna. Circular churches depend from Imperial mausolea of late Antiquity or from the round temple of Minerva Medica. The function of these centrally planned buildings was to concentrate attention on the shrine

15

9. ROME. *S. Stefano Rotondo* (*photo: Italian Institute, London*)

8 or tomb of saint or martyr. S. Costanza was such a rotunda, built in Constantine's lifetime to the memory of his daughter, before his court moved from Rome to Constantinople in 328. This accounts for the pre-Byzantine character of its structure and mosaic decoration. The Roman brick exterior is wholly unadorned and all the splendour resides in the circular arcade within and the mosaic tapestry of the ambulatory vault. An interior ring of twelve coupled columns of smooth granite with composite marble capitals support a boldly defined entablature on high impost blocks. These twin columns—not piers—are linked by broad arches, carrying a cylindrical drum and hemispherical dome whose weight comes down upon the thick concrete outer wall and vaulted passage. The centre with the altar-tomb of the saint is brightly lit by round-headed clerestorey windows. The plain walling in small Roman bricks of drum and dome contrasts with the polychrome splendour of the ambulatory mosaics, divided in twelve geometrical sections and representing delicately writhing vine leaves, abstract patterns or vintage scenes which are pagan rather than Christian. The low ambulatory is sparsely lit from narrow, slanting windows. It has eight niches and four larger recesses facing each other, anticipating the cruciform shape of a Greek-

16

10. ROME. *S. Giovanni in Laterano.* *Baptistery of Constantine*
(*photo: Gabinetto Fotografico Nazionale, Rome*)

cross church. These twelve recesses correspond with the twelve bays of
the arcuated central space.

S. Stefano Rotondo was conceived on a larger scale at the end of **9**
the fifth century (468-83). A circular nave is surrounded by antique
columns with Ionian capitals supporting a horizontal architrave. An
outer ring of columns now forms part of the wall. The mausoleum to
the protomartyr is a vast rotunda with a high cylindrical nave, lit by
numerous windows from the clerestorey and separated by the colonnade
from the lower aisle or ambulatory. Four deep and lofty chapels issue
from here, so that the plan of S. Stefano is a combination of cross and
circle. Martyria and baptisteries of the fourth and fifth centuries were
either circular or polygonal structures. The Lateran Baptistery founded **10**
by Constantine in 325, was reconstructed a century later in octagonal
form. A large circular font in the centre, for baptism by immersion, is
surrounded by eight porphyry columns supporting a straight entablature
(trabeation) and surmounted by another order of columns, forming an
airy canopy beneath the dome. The ambulatory is barrel-vaulted and
the walls of the octagon have marble panelling. Like S. Costanza and S.
Stefano, the Lateran Baptistery receives its light from the clerestorey
windows.

17

11. ROME. *S. Maria in Cosmedin* (*photo: E.N.I.T. Rome*)

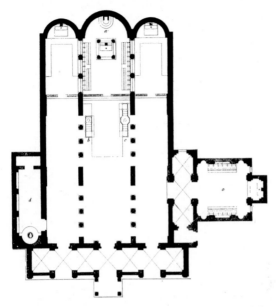

12. ROME. *S. Maria in Cosmedin (from Letarouilly)*

The churches of Medieval Rome take their place beside those of the Early Christian era. So strong was the antique tradition here that neither the Romanesque, nor later the Gothic styles took root. During the iconoclastic period of the eighth and ninth century only three churches were reconstructed, S. Prassede, S. Maria in Domnica and S. Cecilia in Trastevere. An immensely spacious nave of classical proportions and intercolumnation leads towards the wide apse mosaic of S. Maria in Domnica where a Byzantine Virgin is enthroned among a host of angels, white-robed with golden wings. Two minor apses in the ' Syrian ' style terminate the narrow aisles of the church. In S. Prassede piers and columns alternate and the continuous colonnade and horizontal trabeation has been replaced by arcading. Diaphragm arches across the nave support the roof. But the chief glories of these early Medieval churches in Rome are their mosaics: Christ the Judge between Peter and Paul and other saints above a symbolic circle of sheep decorate the apse as in the earlier SS. Cosma and Damiano and in S. Pudenziana.

After the sack of Rome by the Norman Robert Guiscard in 1084, Pope Paschalis II rebuilt several famous basilicas such as Santi Quattro Coronati (1110) with its purist nave-arcade in two tiers, shortened from the original twelve to four columns; S. Saba conspicuous by its oriental, brick-built hemispherical apses without window openings and its division in upper and lower church; S. Maria in Cosmedin (1120-40) with *schola*

13. ROME. *S. Giorgio in Velabro*

cantorum, colonnade and supporting piers, its wide expanse of plain walling intervening between the small clerestorey windows high up beneath the wood roof. There is an open narthex, projecting porch and medieval bell-tower with three-light windows. Brick-built towers with marble colonettes and flat tops are a Roman feature, perhaps influenced by the Lombard campanili and their superimposed sections. Belfries and porticoes like those in S. Giorgio in Velabro, elegantly poised on Ionian columns in front of the sturdy towers in four storeys of tripartite arcading, are characteristic sights of Medieval Rome.

13

14. ROME. *S. Clemente*

The classical module of proportions was frequently altered in later reconstructions. Instead of the nave measuring twice the height of the columns it became narrower, longer and higher. S. Clemente, founded in 380 but rebuilt in the early twelfth century is a case in point. Yet it remains one of the purest and most authentic of Roman churches, incorporating an ancient foundation which was filled in to serve as a base for the new two aisled basilica with its smooth or fluted Ionian columns alternating, its graceful arcades and the famous *schola cantorum* and mosaic pavement enclosed by a low marble screen. The two pulpits on either side of the choir and the canopied altar survive from the ancient basilica. With its geometrical disk pattern, delicate apse mosaic and arcaded forecourt, S. Clemente is one of the most precious and best appointed basilicas in Rome.

S. Maria in Trastevere preserves the width and height of an ancient foundation, though it stems from the Middle Ages (1140) with a rich wooden ceiling, a stout Corinthian colonnade bearing the weight of the clerestorey wall on a straight trabeation. The majestic sanctuary arch and concave apse are enriched by mosaics, and a marble baldacchino shelters the altar. Church architecture in Medieval Rome remained faithful to the Early Christian tradition and even during the Romanesque period preferred the trabeation of classical temples in nave and portico to arcaded structures.

During the second half of the fourth century, Milan frequently

14

21

C

15. MILAN. *S. Lorenzo. Interior with exedrae* (*photo: Costa/E.P.T. Milan*)

was the emperor's residence and, as the See of S. Ambrose, it became one of the religious centres of the West. Some of the monumental churches of that era survive and none more powerful and complex than S. Lorenzo, built around 375 on the vast scale of Imperial Baths or palace architecture. Milanese brick work masonry influenced the early Christian churches of Ravenna and the ' double shell design ' with concave central bays of S. Lorenzo was refined and repeated on a smaller scale in S. Vitale. It was a metropolitan church for the Imperial court with an octagonal central space extending into four wide vaulted niches with two orders of columns screening a gallery above and a passage below. Its central core was encased by an outer wall, leaving room for an ambulatory. Giant corner piers of a later date replacing columns support the grand arches of the four wide exedrae with their double-storeyed loggias. The effect of S. Lorenzo is that of vast spatial breadth with bold hemispherical bays on four sides and an octagonal drum beneath the dome, buttressed by four angular towers reaching no higher than the nave. This compact, richly articulated monument is preceded by an atrium and colonnaded entrance gate.

During the fifth and sixth centuries when Rome fell from power under the barbarian invasions, Ravenna became the creative centre of Early Christian architecture in the West and the depository of Byzantine influences.

16. RAVENNA. *Mausoleum of Galla Placidia*

The Emperor Honorius and Galla Placidia his sister resided in Ravenna, as did Theodoric, king of the Ostrogoths after he had conquered Italy in 476. After Justinian's victory over the Goths, his regents established Byzantine rule in Ravenna and with it the architectural form of imperial court churches such as S. Sergius and Bakchos in Constantinople, polygonal and central, which was to leave its mark on S. Vitale, Ravenna. Thus from about 420 onwards Ravenna absorbed not only the Roman style of baptisteries, mausolea and basilican churches, but increasingly transformed these by overlaying and dissolving wall structures by the colouristic magic of mosaic decoration.

17. RAVENNA. *Orthodox Baptistery (photo: Villani/E.P.T. Ravenna)*

16   Already the Mausoleum of Galla Placidia (*c.* 424), cross-shaped, domed and barrel-vaulted with four arms of equal length was a small jewel on account of its mysterious light effects and mosaic incrustations simulating the starry heavens. Its lower walls are clothed in panels of variegated marble reaching up to the cornices beneath the vaults, and its four niches harbour the huge imperial sarcophagi. The infinitely subtle mosaics of dark turquoise, glittering with gold and emerald, cover the pendentive dome, broad arches and archivolts with geometrical pattern; and the lunettes with images of Apostles, S. Lawrence and the Good Shepherd, lend to the low funerary chapel a mystical aura in stark contrast to the
17   plain brick exterior. The same applies to the Orthodox Baptistery (*c.* 450), an unadorned, two-storeyed octagon without, but a luxuriant interior with superimposed arches framing marble panellings and disks

24

18. RAVENNA. *Tomb of Theodoric*

in the lower zone, windows and feigned niches above and a wealth of delicate mosaic arabesques, obliterating the solid walls and the lightly constructed dome by their colouristic fantasies and thereby enlarging the spatial volume. The large central font is also of octagonal shape. By contrast the Tomb of Theodoric (*c.* 526) is an awesome monument, built **18** of square blocks of Istrian stone, a massive primeval structure carrying a cylindrical drum on a wide polygonal base and a dome built out of a single piece of stone.

But the chief glory of Ravenna is the superb octagonal church of S. Vitale and the two model basilicas dedicated to S. Apollinare. Their simple exteriors of brick and mortar do not prepare the visitor for the refined oriental splendour, and the wealth of mosaics and polychrome marble

19. RAVENNA. S. Apollinare Nuovo (photo: E.P.T. Ravenna)

26

20. RAVENNA. *Basilica of S. Apollinare in Classe*

transfiguring them within. S. Apollinare Nuovo (*c.* 490) is distinctive **19**
for the beauty of its simple nave and infinitely precious columns with
pulvins or impost blocks of inverted cone shape above the capitals from
which the arches are sprung. The Byzantine rows of martyrs and holy
Virgins, static and frontal along the broad horizontal planes beneath the
clerestorey, but above all the Three Kings from the East speed on in relentless rhythm towards the altar. Mosaics relating Christ's life and Passion
in the topmost register complete the transformation of the walls into an
insubstantial Eastern luxuriance. S. Apollinare Nuovo differs from a
Roman basilica by the wider nave relative to its length and by the courtly
style of Byzantium.

Less rich but even more solemn is S. Apollinare in Classe (532-49), the **20**
former port of Ravenna at the edge of the pineta; its planar exterior is
composed of oblong shapes, cubes and triangles with blind arcades
framing the double row of windows. Geometrical bodies like the projecting rooms beside the polygonal apse—curved within—the elegantly
arcaded narthex and the detached cylindrical tower enhance the plain
brick exterior of the church. Such basic simplicity without, is matched
by a spacious interior, a wide nave with twenty-four columns of Grecian
marble on square pedestals supporting oriental pulvins and arches and a
profusion of windows in clerestorey, apse and narrow aisles. The apse
mosaic of S. Apollinare standing amidst his flock in the ancient attitude

27

21. RAVENNA. *Basilica of S. Vitale. Mosaics*

22. RAVENNA. *Basilica of S. Vitale. Mosaics in apse*

of prayer beneath the great dark cross is the principal Byzantine ornament in this Justinian basilica.

The supreme achievement of Justinian architecture is the centrally planned octagonal church of S. Vitale in Ravenna (546-48), a compact

21, 22

23. TORCELLO. *Cathedral of S. Maria Assunta*

and intricate organism, famed for its courtly mosaics portraying the
Emperor and his wife Theodora bringing gifts to the altar. A building
of such sublimity of spatial configurations and spiritual momentum is
unique in Western art and its magic can never be conveyed in words.
Erected by western artists after Justinian's conquest of Italy from the
Ostrogoths, it is close in style to Byzantine imperial churches. Its
exterior of warm brick colour, its planar surfaces, terracotta cornices and
pilaster supports reflect the complex cubic volumes within, but not the
rarefied splendour of marble revetments and mosaics. The octagonal
drum of the dome sits squarely upon the wider and lower roofs of the
nave and ambulatory with a narthex placed asymmetrically, and flanked
by apses instead of being on the main axis of the building. Arcaded
windows in two storeys and supporting buttresses at the angles divide
the exterior into geometrical planes.

This organised system of planes conceals a curvilinear interior of
incomparable complexity and splendour. Here the central octagon
dominates, opening into the darker ambulatory by means of recessed,
concave and vaulted spaces between lofty piers supporting narrow arches.
These are surmounted by the clerestorey with large windows in every
bay. Upper and lower zones form semicircular niches divided by triple
arches and columns. Some of these have flat sloping capitals with
perforated lacework design on a dark ground and a carved pulvin of
Byzantine type. The octagonal nave, radiating and withdrawing into

24. TORCELLO. *S. Fosca*

seven bays, culminates on the eighth side in the oblong presbytery and apse, flanked by two circular vestries. Here along the entrance arch to the altar zone are the roundels of Christ and the twelve apostles; the side wall glitters with the jewelled and solemn portraits of the Emperor Justinian and his court and in the golden conch of the apse is a beardless Christ-Apollo enthroned between archangels, S. Vitale and the founder-bishop Ecclesius presenting a model of his church. Thus S. Vitale with its central core and alternating rhythm of projecting piers and retreating niches, mysteriously linked in a continuous flow and ornate with the luxuriance of coloured, light-reflecting mosaics and inlaid marble, denies and transfigures all structural solidity. Yet this airy interior with its unexpected vistas is clothed by a geometrical shell, echoing and screening the spatial divisions within.

Links with the Byzantine architects of Ravenna were strong in the Veneto, especially in the lonely island of Torcello in the lagoons. Here the Cathedral of S. Maria Assunta, the Lombard bell-tower with its decorative arcading and the octagonal church of S. Fosca form an incom-

25. MURANO. *Cathedral of SS. Maria e Donato*

23 parable triad. The Cathedral, rebuilt in 863 and 1008, is a spacious basilica, its nave and wide marble pavement separated from the sanctuary by an iconostasis on antique columns and by a parapet of four Byzantine reliefs of heraldic beasts and arabesques. From the golden apse the tall and haunting shape of the Madonna Orans dominates the church, remote and solitary.

24 Next to the Cathedral is the beautifully shaped Greek-cross church of S. Fosca (1011) with its broad eight-sided base and outer portico and its cylindrical crown—only two rings of the original dome survive— squatting firmly upon the four arms of the cross. The narrow and stilted arches of the external passage are echoed in the window openings of the gabled apses beneath the hemispherical drum. In its dignified calm, compactness and shapeliness, S. Fosca has a mosque-like appearance.

25 In the same context belongs the Cathedral of SS. Maria e Donato at Murano. Its apse of about 1150 is richer, wider and more articulate. The Lombard motive of superimposed loggias is enhanced by the pictorial

26. VENICE. *Basilica of S. Mark's*

effects of white marble upon brick and terracotta, mirrored in the water. Twin columns, balusters and arcades lighten the weight of solid walls as well as other surface ornaments, without weakening the broad unity of the Byzantine structure.

Venice, in close contact with the eastern Empire, combines the splendour of the Orient with the Roman heritage of Western Europe. The hemispherical domes of S. Mark's Cathedral raised on drums are Byzantine, but the broad round arches and square piers supporting clearly defined vaults are basically western Romanesque. Yet this cruciform, five-domed basilica with its effusion of mosaics, marble inlays, **26**

27. VENICE. *Basilica of S. Mark's. Gallery*

rich capitals and sculptural decorations breathes the luxuriance of the East. The church was founded in 864 to receive the body of S. Mark, reconstructed between 1042-85 over a Greek-cross plan and enlarged and adorned far into the sixteenth century and beyond. Byzantine, Romanesque and Gothic styles, contributed, without altering the original Eastern concept of a domed central space and a subsidiary dome over each arm of the cross. The pendentive dome is carried on huge angular piers, arcaded on two levels. The dominant motive is thus the grand succession of airy cavities of the cupolas along the main axis, glittering with the golden background of the mosaics. The interior of S. Mark's overawes by its huge dimensions, its solid masses of domical shapes, its great tunnel vaults and clear spatial divisions. It is an intersection of two gigantic halls with the crossing lit from windows cut into the dome; the nave is extended eastwards towards the apse and westwards towards the narthex. Altar zone and apse are raised and screened by an iconostasis. Rows of niches and colonnades and giant archways articulate the nave, though the galleries above are mere balconies or passageways. The gaunt and elongated 27 figures of the mosaics from Old Testament and Christological cycle cover the planes and curvatures of the walls, and their burnished gold sheathes them in an aura of mystery and subdued light.

The powerful masses and simple volumes of the interior contrast starkly with the over-ornateness of S. Mark's façade and its five deeply set portals leading into the narthex. The central porch has the widest span with superimposed triple arches, flanked by two orders of columns, some with Byzantine capitals. A large tympanum mosaic is circumscribed by an ornamental frieze. A second storey of blind arcades and a central window with balusters, mosaics, turrets and figurative sculpture screens but does not impair the Byzantine character of the Basilica. The ornamental superstructure of florid cusps, pinnacles and ogee arches of the International Gothic blend harmoniously with the Romanesque elements of the façade and the graded Byzantine domes and bulbous lanterns. Moreover, the four Hellenistic bronze horses on the façade terrace, proclaim the diversity of Venetian civilisation.

CHAPTER TWO

ROMANESQUE ARCHITECTURE 1050-1250

Romanesque architecture in Italy has two principal sources, one in the north, and the other centred in the Kingdom of the Two Sicilies. The Lombard style, related to the German Romanesque, spread from Como, Milan, Pavia to the cities of Emilia (Modena, Parma), and even as far south as Bari in Apulia. Its power potential was expressed in large spatial units and generous rounded forms—broad arches, cylindrical apses and heavy rib-vaults—or in geometrical and planar surfaces, often overlaid with sculptural relief ornament. Tuscany is a case apart. The octagonal Baptistery at Florence is in the Roman and Early Christian tradition. Its facings of coloured marble and those of S. Miniato determine the Florentine church facades of the Quattrocento. The cathedrals of Pisa and Lucca with their delicate colonettes and superimposed arcading display an oriental luxuriance. In Sicily and Apulia the Norman style massive and regal, blends with Saracen pointed arches, Byzantine mosaic decoration and Muslim domes.

The Romanesque style in Italy is the most powerful aesthetic manifestation since Graeco-Roman antiquity. Under the influence of Teutonic forces in the north, Byzantine in the south of the peninsula, it evolved out of early Christian and late Roman art. The basilica remained the canonical form of ecclesiastical buildings with regional variations according to whether the local contacts were with France and Germany or with the countries of the eastern Mediterranean. Great trading centres like Venice or Pisa and the crusader ports in Apulia transmitted the Byzantine and Islamic spirit. North and central Italy developed the Lombard and Tuscan Romanesque, whereas the kingdom of the Two Sicilies under Norman and Hohenstaufen rule was open to the influence from the Eastern Empire. Rome remained artistically barren during the middle ages, except for cloisters, belfries and the work of the Cosmati in inlaid marble. The creative activity was concentrated in the rising city-communes of the north, vigorously fighting for independence, while in Apulia and Sicily the Norman conquest of the eleventh century left a trail of magnificent buildings, cathedrals, convents, castles, royal chapels and palaces.

But the cradle of Romanesque art was in Lombardy. S. Abbondio and S. Fedele in Como, S. Ambrogio in Milan set the pace in monumental edifices organizing massive stone structures into clearly defined spatial units. Thick walls with few openings, twin towers, round apses, cylindrical columns and composite piers, supporting nave-arcades and aisle-galleries, a colonnaded crypt beneath a raised presbytery, atrium or narthex in front of the façade, these are some of the structural elements of the Romanesque basilica. As the Gothic strives after transcendental height by vertical orientation, slender shafts and multiple rib-vaulting, so the Romanesque is anchored to the earth, favours breadth and horizontality, the rounded forms of arch and apse and pillar, a static equilibrium. By the middle of the twelfth century the Lombard style had spread to Emilia, Tuscany and Umbria, creating monumental churches in Pavia, Bergamo and Brescia, in Parma and Modena, Assisi and Spoleto and above all in Pisa, each with its individual character like the coloured marble façades of Florence, the many-pillared loggias of Pisa, the gabled screen façade of S. Michele, Pavia or the majestic lion porches of Emilia. Separate belfry and baptistery form with the cathedral a grand compound of ecclesiastical buildings in Pisa, Parma and Cremona.

Whereas the northern and central Italian Romanesque is massive and sober, though lightened by decorative detail such as arcading, rose-windows and sculptural ornament, the cathedrals on the Mediterranean shore like Amalfi and Salerno were colourful and gay, open to Moorish influences. But it is in Apulia and Sicily where western and eastern civilisations meet and the regal style of the Normans is grafted upon the Graeco-Roman, Byzantine and Muslim legacy in a powerful group of domed cathedrals or in the polygonal castles and block-like palaces of the Hohenstaufen Emperor Frederick II. His dream of a supra-national Italy, integral part of the Holy Roman Empire, broke on the rock of papal resistance and Anjou henchmen. Frederick died in 1250. By then the Early Gothic style, introduced by the Cistercians and adopted by the Friars Minor, had begun to replace the ' monumental magnificence ' of the mature Romanesque.

S. Ambrogio, in Milan, is the weighty and sombre mother church of **28** Romanesque Lombardy. Built during the eleventh century over a fourth century foundation, and vaulted in the early twelfth, S. Ambrogio is essentially an Early Christian basilica. The arcaded atrium forms a spacious rectangular prelude to the narthex with a wide gabled frontage of classical arches in two tiers whose largest in the centre ascends towards the apex of the triangle. The façade windows are one source of light in the majestic interior. Two square towers flank the narthex of the church; the lofty canon's tower on the left has five sections divided horizontally by cornices and corbels and vertically by pilaster strips. Medieval towers, classical atrium and blind arcading on the west-front are an austere preparation for the ponderous nave and square bays within. Broad ribs issue from the composite corner-piers supporting the domical vaults. The twin bays with their wide arches embracing four minor ones are supported by piers which also carry the vaults and walls of the nave without a clerestorey. The groin-vaulted aisles are only half the width

28. MILAN. *Basilica of S. Ambrogio*

of the nave. The upward thrust of piers and diagonal ribs under the wide span of the Roman arches and their weight-bearing function are harmoniously balanced and this accounts for the impression of gravity and power of the interior. The nave divides into four square sections, rib-vaulted, except for the polygonal dome over the crossing. The interior
29 of S. Ambrogio impresses by its structural as well as its aesthetic coherence, the quadripartite division of bays with the smaller arches of the women's galleries, the broad transverse arches spanning the nave and the powerful combination of multiple pilasters and half columns.

The main constituents of the Romanesque style in Lombardy are exemplified here: articulation and division of mass; square, ponderous bays conjoined with boldly swung arches with rib-vaulting in the nave, groin-vaulted in the aisles; generous rounded shapes, carried on giant piers; sparing decorative carvings on capitals, archivolts and friezes. In the squat and primeval strength of its interior S. Ambrogio is northern in form and in spirit.

30 Besides metropolitan Milan, Como was the most influential centre of Lombard architecture. Its vast basilican church of S. Abbondio outside the city walls (1063-95) has five aisles and a majestic round apse, flanked by twin towers. The sheer grandeur of the church is in its massive pile, the long stepped roof, extended sanctuary and towering apse. A forest of simple stone pillars with moulded capitals activates the lofty interior whose breadth is reflected in the wide sweep of the façade, where applied pilasters and half-columns demarcate nave and

29. MILAN. *Basilica of S. Ambrogio. Interior*

lateral aisles. Lombard roof arcading and relief carving around windows
are the sparing ornaments. A wood ceiling covers the main body of the
church, but northern rib-vaulting the sanctuary and apse. Craftsmen
from Lake Como carried their style to Bergamo, Brescia, Pavia and deep
into Emilia and Tuscany.

Bergamo can boast the Romanesque Basilica of S. Maria Maggiore, **31**
built between 1137-87 on a Latin-cross plan. Lombard in style with
miniature arcading, it has a three-tier lion portico on slender shafts in
Veronese marble with animal reliefs and figure sculpture. The exterior
of the apse and the octagonal drum-cupola with bipartite openings above
and a gyrating open arcade between semicircular string-course mouldings
and the tall, deeply recessed windows with colonettes attached to pilasters
are a squat yet elegant composition.

30. COMO. *Basilica of S. Abbondio*

31. BERGAMO. *Basilica of S. Maria Maggiore. Detail*

32   A landmark of the Lombard Romanesque is S. Michele, Pavia, where the Emperor Frederick II was crowned. The gabled façade in three parts with its lofty vertical divisions and triple doorways serves as a screen for nave and aisles. An arcaded gallery occurs under the roof. This and the clustered half-columns running the whole height of the façade, sparing window-openings, recessed portals within multiple arches, and horizontal strips of fabulous sculpture in the greyish gold sandstone **33** make up an austere design. The monumental interior has a raised sanctuary above the crypt and an octagonal dome on double squinches over the crossing. Its square bays are formed by clustered piers which carry the arches and ribs of the vault. The original clerestorey is now a women's gallery and the well-defined transept projects beyond the aisles. The apse terminates in one quadripartite bay.

34   Another basilica of great distinction in the Lombard plain is S. Zeno Maggiore in Verona, also built during the middle of the twelfth century. The façade has a great wheel window beneath the gable and a projecting lion porch of red marble in the lofty central rectangle masking the nave. The frontage is scanned vertically by thin pilaster strips. Figurative reliefs from Genesis flank the porch. The two-aisled interior **35** is of great power and solemnity. Compound piers indicating the bays alternate with columnar shafts, firmly planted on square stone bases. No women's gallery breaks into the massive walls, only a tentative clerestorey with narrow windows under the flat wooden roof. Beneath the choir parapet, cutting across the whole width of the nave, three dark cavities lead into the splendid crypt under the raised presbytery which is reached by a flight of stairs from the aisles. The apsidal east end is flanked by a proudly soaring tower.

     In Emilia pride of place belongs to the Romanesque cathedrals of Parma and Modena, both from the early twelfth century with Piacenza and Ferrara following in quick succession. The triforium arches on the **36** exterior walls of Modena Cathedral, begun in 1099, are perhaps a reflection of the Pisan wealth of arcading so that it appears a compound of Tuscan and Lombard styles. The Modena façade with its towering central section, independent of the nave, is richly articulated; the buttressing pilasters and two-tier porch projecting strongly. The portal, carried on slender columns, rests upon lions, a motif found in Apulia. Four large panels with biblical reliefs are let into the façade. Carved capitals, doorjambs and friezes are by the stark and primitive master Wiligelmo. The famous choir screen with the Last Supper by Anselmo da Campione is of later date. Two short turrets over the gabled façade correspond with two others over the east end of the church. The square and massive belfry, the Torre Ghirlandina is articulated by six storeys and graded

32. PAVIA. *S. Michele (photo: Chiolini/E.P.T. Pavia)*

33. Pavia. *S. Michele (photo: Chiolini/E.P.T. Pavia)*

windows. Three apses, blind arcading and sculptural ornament enhance this basically geometric design of rectilinear and semicircular shapes.

During the thirteenth century the timber roof was replaced by a Gothic vault. The transept does not project beyond the aisles and the interior space is lucidly divided into four square bays contained within the massive double arches. In place of a woman's gallery there is a low

37

44

34. VERONA. *S. Zeno Maggiore (photo: R.I.B.A. Collection)*

triforium in the second storey. The main piers link up with the wall by supporting arches reaching across the aisles. The grand climax is the rich choir screen separating nave and chancel with columns carried by lions and human grotesques. Access to the sanctuary is by a flight of steps from each aisle. Externally the great rose window, continuous arcading and fine portals as well as sculptured panels, archivolts, door-jambs enrich the planar aspect of the church.

One of the finest groups of ecclesiastical buildings—cathedral, belfry, baptistery—is to be found in nearby Parma. The Cathedral **38-40** rebuilt after the earthquake of 1117, has a façade not unlike that of S. Michele, Pavia, a broad gabled front with two tiers of triforium arches and ascending arcade beneath the cornice. The vertical is stressed by the projecting main portal, also in two tiers, with colonettes resting on couchant lions, and by the shaft buttresses framing the arched window. More complex is the external aspect of the Cathedral from the apsidal

45

35. VERONA. *S. Zeno Maggiore. Interior*

back where the identical cubes of transept and presbytery with the semi-spherical apses and the octagonal drum-cupola form a compound of geometrical bodies. The large planes of the building are diversified by high oblong panelling below and the continuous loggias above. The interior with its warm red-brick colouring consists of a spacious nave with lofty rib-vaulting, supported by round arches springing from the shafts of the piers. The bays of nave and aisles are square and the tri-forium gallery beneath the clerestorey has four arches in each bay. The raised presbytery is reached by a broad flight of steps extending across the whole width of the nave. A groin-vaulted and many-columned crypt occupies the whole area beneath transept and sanctuary. The cupola over the crossing is supported on squinches and enhanced by Correggio's illusionist painting of the Assumption.

41   To the south-west of the Cathedral stands Antelami's baptistery, famed for its sculpture and begun in 1196. It shares with its Florentine prototype the octagonal shape and the straight architraves over the columns, but five-part loggias divide each face of the monument. Its overall effect is totally different from that of the Florentine Baptistery on account of these four sets of galleries above the wide span of massive blind arcades on ground level and the broad flat buttresses at the corners, crowned by pinnacles. The medieval Romanesque is lightened by the slender colonettes and arcaded galleries, crowned by a top storey of seven

36. MODENA. *Cathedral*

37. Modena. *Cathedral. Interior*

slender arches beneath the overhanging cornice. The three portals are deeply recessed and their tympana bear Antelami's figure sculpture or reliefs. The interior is sixteen-sided with a ribbed vault, a two-tier loggia, niches and altar recess. Figures representing the Labours of the Months are placed all round the interior walls of the Baptistery which has the geometrical clarity of the Lombard Romanesque.

Though Florence is pre-eminently a city of the Early Renaissance, it is graced by two monuments whose basic geometrical design and polychrome marble panelling are of the eleventh century: the Basilica of S. Miniato al Monte and the monumental Baptistery facing the Cathedral—Dante's *mio bel S. Giovanni* (Inf. XIX, 17). The lattter has a Roman foundation of the fifth century, suggested by its octagonal form, Corinthian columns and twin pilasters, bearing the weight of the architrave and the grand triumphal arch of the shallow altar recess which was once of apsidal form. These classical elements are characteristic of the Florentine proto-Renaissance of the eleventh and twelfth century. The Baptistery measures ninety feet across the floor and its vast cupola weighs down upon the octagonal attic storey and the perimeter walls. A pitched roof covers the exterior of the cupola which is decorated with Byzantine mosaics within. The structural weight-bearing stresses are resolved by the external zebra buttresses at the eight corners and the free-standing trabeated columns and corner pilasters inside. But aesthetically the main feature is the geometrical patterning of marble inlay—green upon white—rectangular and semicircular facets and the three blind arcades

42

48

38. PARMA. *Cathedral, Bell-tower and Baptistery*

39. PARMA. *Cathedral*

40. PARMA. *Cathedral. Principal nave*

41. PARMA. *Baptistery. Detail of vaulted ceiling*

42. FLORENCE. *Baptistery*

43. FLORENCE. *S. Miniato al Monte* (*photo: Italian Institute, London*)

on each side of the octagon. Beneath the windows there is a semi-abstract design of mock arcading and in the second storey of the interior a false bifora gallery. The springing of the vault starts from a band of squares in polychrome marble. Thus the organic and static aspect of the building, stressed by architectural members, is masked by marble and mosaic decoration. Geometrical clarity and diversity lend to the walls of the octagon lightness and abstract purity, without impairing the impression of mass and of weight.

This Florentine rationale based upon the mathematical forms like square, triangle and semicircle was to attain its perfect expression in the façade of S. Miniato al Monte. It hails from the twelfth century, though the basilica was completed by 1062. There is no more lucid and well

43

44. FLORENCE. *S. Miniato al Monte. Interior*

defined church front in Florence, and variations of it multiplied throughout the Renaissance. There are two storeys and a gabled summit; two orders; the central section marking the nave, the half pediments the aisles. The five identical arches between half columns with composite capitals are classical and serene, only slightly recessed, enframing doors and oblong panels of coloured marble with sparing ornament. The mosaic above the central window is of later date as is the more elaborate patterning of **44** the gable. The interior of the basilica follows the Lombard usage with aisles lower than the nave, an open truss roof, brightly painted, arcades and clerestorey, strengthened by piers and arches, spanning the nave in an even rhythm after every third bay.

The presbytery of S. Miniato is raised high and reached by a long flight of steps from each aisle. A resplendent marble screen and pulpit with carved figures, rosettes and lace work ornament reaching from pier to pier cut off the presbytery. The crypt is at the level of the nave. Rounded apse and interior walls have geometrical marble inlays in black and white, mainly diamonds within square or circle. A special feature is the tesselated pavement, great wheels of mosaic with abstract designs, encircling heraldic beasts and the signs of the zodiac. S. Miniato is the

45. PISA. *Cathedral and Campanile*

only Romanesque basilica in Florence, utterly refined and sumptuous, yet of great clarity and perfect equipoise. An even light from the clerestorey windows suffuses the church and the diaphragm arches across the wood ceiling are a prelude to the vaulting system of later basilican churches.

The most spectacular building complex in Italy besides the Piazza of S. Marco and also indebted to eastern influences is the Cathedral Close of Pisa. S. Miniato was of pure Tuscan lineage with Roman architectural elements, Pisa Cathedral—in its incomparable setting between the **45** leaning tower, Baptistery and the Gothic Camposanto—with its decorative profusion is akin to Arabian examples. The Cathedral was founded in 1063 after a victory of the Pisan fleet over the Saracens at Palermo. Its Greek architect Buscheto planned it as a five aisled Basilica with transepts, lofty walls, colonnaded arcading and a flat timber roof. Consecrated in 1121 by Pope Gelasius, the nave of the Cathedral was lengthened between 1250 and 1270 by the architect Rainaldus who created the west front and raised the elliptical cupola over the crossing.

The two single-aisled transepts with their own apses, intersecting the nave are in themselves like smaller cathedrals within the larger unit. **46** Pointed dome and triumphal arch are not Gothic but Saracen, as are many of the external ornaments, lozenges and patens and flat pilasters clinging closely to the marble panellings of the walls. Colonnades and galleries continue all around the building so that the interior space affords a variety of unexpected views. Even the transepts are screened from the nave by bridge-like galleries over arcades, made more conspicuous by the black and white banding of marble. Columns, capitals and arches are Roman, and the latter spring from square impost blocks. The exterior of Pisa Cathedral is of even greater monumentality and magnificence

55

46. PISA. *Cathedral. Interior looking east*

by dint of the serried rows of loggias and blind arcading which were of
paramount influence on other Tuscan churches, and more especially
in neighbouring Lucca, Pistoia and further south in Arezzo.   At
47 Pisa the leaden roofs over the multiple aisles, transepts, apses build up
towards the climax of the cupola, ringed by its cusped Gothic gallery.
The great pile of the building dominates the Cathedral Close not only
by its golden marble panelling and disk and rhomboid ornaments, but as
a structural synthesis of intersecting longitudinal bodies with apsidal

47. PISA. *Cathedral. Apse*

and gabled ends rising in three storeys towards the crowning cupola. The thirteenth century façade with its multiplicity of open loggias reaching up to the gabled summit became a feature of the Pisan style. Here the richly moulded cornices, capitals and small arches, standing free of the wall and the ensuing play of light and shadow are of singular grace and, together with marble inlays and incrustations and bronze doors, endow the Pisan façade with a richness and radiance which are a fusion of oriental and Mediterranean civilisation.

The Leaning Tower, begun in 1174, is in stylistic harmony with the **48** adjacent cathedral: blind arcading below with lozenge ornaments in the upper sections of the arches and six concentric rings of detached loggias on shafts with a cylindrical belfry of smaller circumference account for the elegance and classical uniformity.

Less unified externally is the Baptistery, a rotunda with a huge hemi- **49** spherical dome overlaid with Gothic finials and pointed arches in the upper registers above the Romanesque arcading of the ground storey. The Baptistery, begun by Diotisalvi in 1152 has a noble interior of classical sobriety, recalling S. Stefano Rotondo and S. Costanza in its circular nave, separated from its cross-vaulted ambulatory by a ring of piers and of columns supporting a gallery high above the groundfloor arcades. A large octagonal font with a figure of the Baptist by Giovanni Pisano

57

48. PISA. *The Campanile or Leaning Tower*

49. PISA. *Baptistery*

dominates the centre. Sculptured busts by the same artist, formerly in the corbelled triangles of the exterior, are now displayed along the interior walls. Chief glory of the Baptistery, apart from the Roman severity of its interior is the pulpit by Nicola Pisano, his first known work of *c.* 1260, and here the primitive power of early Romanesque sculpture is redeemed by the classical stance and humanity of the figures.

The Camposanto at Pisa, designed in 1278 by Giovanni da Simone, **50** forms a foil to the resplendent compound of the Cathedral Close. It is an open rectangle, a cloister around a central greensward, and its grace and serenity are based upon the continuous sequence of round arches, filled-in during the fifteenth century with Gothic quatrefoil tracery and colonettes. The Romanesque arches are supported by angular piers and the stone tracery within is set back in space, resting on a high podium

59

50. PISA. *Camposanto*

which is interrupted only at the entrance grates. In the Camposanto
Romanesque gravity blends with Gothic weightlessness and it is in the
cloistered peace, the ordered symmetry, the play of light and of line that
its architectural beauty resides, an enclosed aerial space under the open
sky where walls are dissolved by elegant openings within the harmonious
proportions of a classical atrium.

Romanesque arcading of the Pisan kind spread to the neighbouring
subject city of Lucca and most sumptuously to the Cathedral of S.
51 Martino, focal centre of a spacious square. Here three storeys of external
loggias display an oriental luxuriance in their deeply carved capitals and
cornices, the shafts decked with animal sculpture or spiral fluting, alternating with smooth columns inlaid with geometrical patterns of coloured
stone. These delicate loggias rise above the three powerful Roman arches
of the narthex on massive piers with the famous group of S. Martin and
the beggar in one of the spandrels. The façade by Giudetto dates from
1204 with Lombard craftsmen from the Como area responsible for the
52 ornateness of the carving. S. Michele in Foro is likewise decorated with
free-standing arcaded galleries, building up in four tiers to a gabled
summit of quite exceptional height. The third and oldest of Romanesque
churches in Lucca is S. Frediano (1112-47), a five-aisled basilica with a
perfectly cylindrical apse in two-coloured stone with a temple-like
superstructure of slender Ionic pillars supporting a straight entablature.
This classical feature is flanked by a towering campanile—as is the
façade of S. Martino—a square prismatic shape with graded openings
in all six registers over a solid base, narrow arched cavities, divided by
shafts.

51. LUCCA. *Cathedral of S. Martino*

52. Lucca. *S. Michele in Foro*

The style of Pisa and Lucca extended to Pistoia and further south **53** to Arezzo. In Pistoia's S. Giovanni Fuoricivitas of 1170, marble bands in two colours screen the sides of the church, a chromatic horizontal network masking walls, pilasters and applied arches in three superimposed rows. The lofty blind arcades with diamond shapes under the arches pointing upwards and a decorative centre of square or paten are an imitation of those in Pisa Cathedral, as are the upper rows of open arcading. But their banding and their proportions make them appear heavier.

53. PISTOIA. *S. Giovanni Fuoricivitas*

54. AREZZO. *S. Maria della Pieve*

55. SPOLETO. *Basilica of S. Eufemia. Interior*

56. SPOLETO. *Basilica of S. Eufemia. Sacred ornamental column (or praying column)*

The parish church of Arezzo (the Pieve) of 1216 is a provincial 54 version of the style developed in Lucca but far less sophisticated. Three horizontal rows of loggias crowd in upon the upper storeys of the façade above a solid basement where portals alternate with blind arcades. The play of light and of shade and a sculptural sensivity enhance the exterior of these Romanesque churches in Tuscany.

The Umbrian hill towns of Assisi and Spoleto also have magnificent Romanesque churches. The powerful duchy of Spoleto was founded by the Lombards in the sixth century and later became a fief of Charlemagne. Its dukes governed Umbria and the Marches throughout the middle-ages until Innocent II incorporated these into the papal state. The many churches of Spoleto reflect the development from Early Christian to late medieval times. S. Salvatore has a massive domical apse and fluted columns with Corinthian capitals bearing a heavy architrave like a Roman temple. The tenth century church of S. Eufemia, now part of the bishop's 55, 56 palace, is a courtly medieval building of exceptional height and impeccable interior articulation. The early Romanesque brick structure was probably the palatine chapel of the dukes. Its long shafts, running up from the ground to the vault without a break and the tall and narrow apse both emphasize height. Powerful block capitals on sturdy piers carry the round arches and an unusually spacious women's gallery above. S. Eufemia is a three-aisled basilica where weight is overcome by height and primitive force refined by a noble restraint. The symmetry of arcade-supports in two tiers and the tall rectangular bays enclosing twin arches, separated by the long half columns, are the means by which space is scanned.

The façade of S. Pietro—besides that of Spoleto's S. Maria Assunta 57 —is in the Umbrian style of the thirteenth century. It is distinguished by geometrical divisions of squares and rectangles in three storeys, crowned by a pediment and adorned by relief panels. The main entrance has a large horseshoe tympanum and, like the flanking portals, is guarded by crouching animals. Six oblong panels containing sculptures of fighting beasts and other ornaments overlay the planar surfaces on either side of the porch. A large round window within a square frame in stone is the geometrical centre of this splendid façade whose storeys are separated by string courses and miniature arcading.

The façade of S. Rufino (Assisi) is of regal dignity in its judiciously 58 placed ornaments and tripartite division: a pointed arch running the whole height of the building with a rose window supported by small angel figures above the richly carved main portal; portal and rose window are repeated on a smaller scale to the left and right of the central arch. A dwarf gallery and a double string course or corbel table cut across the

57. SPOLETO. *S. Pietro*

58. ASSISI. *Cathedral of S. Rufino*

F

59. Tuscania (*Viterbo*). *S. Pietro*

60. CASTEL SANT'ELIA (*Viterbo*). *The Basilica*

façade and its pilaster-strips, dividing it into squares and oblongs—a unified whole, an exalted geometry. Pointed arch and gable are countered by a squat rectangular campanile standing beside the church. S. Rufino was built in the mid-twelfth century.

Other resplendent façades of the Romanesque occur in Etruria and more especially in the ancient town of Tuscania, near Viterbo. A central rose window and small arcaded gallery supporting a corbelled cornice recur in S. Pietro as do the three portals; but the sculptural **59** decoration is richer and heavier than at Assisi and no planar surface is left unadorned. Figures from Inferno, medallions with apostolic emblems and heraldic beasts in low relief overlay the central section of the façade. S. Maria Maggiore is similarly constructed; but here the portals are deeply recessed with multiple arches and the sculpture is found in the tympana. The two basilicas in Tuscania, ensconced on their ancient necropolis are the quintessence of Etruscan, medieval and Roman civilisations. Their massive façades, richly articulated by dwarf galleries, portals, windows and sculptures have lost the lightness of the Pisan

61. Castel Sant'Elia. *Basilica. Interior*

arcading, and the flat gable has replaced the triangular Lombard. The interior is no less solemn and majestic than the façade. In S. Pietro a broad nave under a timber roof is framed by stone columns and Roman arches with square bases and impost-blocks. The raised sanctuary ends in a tripartite apse. A stark primeval simplicity and strength prevail, whereas the splendid crypt under the presbytery is distinguished by its many small columns supporting a vaulted ceiling.

60 In the wild Sabine mountains north of Rome the small solitary Basilica of Castel Sant'Elia in the shadow of a rocky escarpment hails from the early eleventh century. It is a plain, brick-built priory church of the Cluniac order with nave, aisles, transepts and rounded apse, clearly and soberly designed. The façade is equally simple with few Lombard ornaments: a recessed central doorway with high tympanum beneath the enclosing arch, flanked by two smaller ones; arcading under the eaves stresses the stepped roofs of the aisles and the base of the
61 pediment. Antique columns of mottled marble within, support rough masonry arches; there are small windows and a concave apse, frescoed with Byzantine paintings of Christ the Judge. Castel Sant'Elia is a rustic church set in romantic isolation over a deep ravine, unscathed relic of primitive times, compounded of basic geometrical shapes.

62 Further south the Cathedral of Caserta Vecchia near Capua built on a hill side dominating a small fortified town (1120-1153) is a Norman edifice with marked Saracen influence in the interlacing arches and polychrome patterning of the central cupola. The two tiers of blind arcading,

62. CASERTA VECCHIA. *Cathedral*

the pointed arches evolved long before the Gothic by intersecting two round ones, give to the octagonal drum and its abstract ornamentation in two-colour mosaics an oriental aspect. Inside, light floods the space beneath the cupola with its radiation of ribs and blind arcading. The nave arches on Corinthian columns lead towards the lofty apse under the dome, reached by a broad flight of stairs. This is the northernmost Norman cathedral in Italy, impressive synthesis of Moorish ornament and shallow cupola with Romanesque structure, heralding the massive and elegant Norman churches and palaces of Apulia and Sicily.

Romanesque architecture in southern Italy was centred in the Salernitano, Apulia and Sicily. Its principal agents were the Normans. By 1070 Robert Guiscard had advanced as far as Salerno and made it his capital and by the end of the century his rule was established in Apulia

73

63. SALERNO. *Cathedral tower*

and Sicily.
Saracen, By
atrium wit
of stilted a
campanile
Amalfi on
succumbec
Its picture
Baroque s
arches in
mosaic de
Ravello in
and here tl
with lion
chief attra
  In th
built mor
walls arti
cupolas,
churches
S. Sabin
square s

64.   AMALFI (*Salerno*).   *Cathedral*

67. TRANI. *Cathedral*

68. TRANI. *Cathedral. Interior*

sheer. The spacious nave has a wood roof, but the aisles are vaulted;
a triforium gallery under enclosing arches and a lofty iconostasis at arcade
level in front of triumphal arch and octagonal cupola, a well lit transept
and shallow apse complete this Norman pilgrimage church of impressive
dimensions.

Trani Cathedral has one of the finest crypts in southern Italy. This
cross-vaulted, four-aisled crypt with a veritable forest of Greek marble
columns was the original eighth century church upon which the upper
church was built by the Normans in 1094. The resplendent west front
with a stepped gable and a loggia across the façade, was preceded by a
double stairway intended for a covered portico. A most elegant campanile
adjoining, rises in five sections with graduated lights upon a massive base,
pierced by a tall pointed arch. The included transept is flush with the
aisles, and its lofty arcades and three projecting apses stress the immense

67, 68

69. TROIA (*Foggia*). *Cathedral*

70. MOLFETTA (*Bari*). *Cathedral*

height of the building. The interior has double columns to support the nave walls, triforium and clerestorey. Trani Cathedral with its gleaming façade close to the seashore and in sight of Hohenstaufen castle is of incomparable beauty.

A perfect example of a smaller Romanesque cathedral is in the Apulian hill town of Troia, with blind arcading all round and disks and **69** diamonds carved into the walls below arch level as in the Cathedral at Pisa. The façade was begun in 1093. But the weightier upper storey with the magnificent wheel window and marble facings, the richly carved archivolt and framing arch on paired columns are of the twelfth and thirteenth centuries. The two lions squatting on the ornamental cornice are Norman in their latent force and fierceness.

Molfetta Cathedral, set like Trani at the water's edge, has a planar **70** body with a pair of slender towers at the east and a succession of three cupolas along the nave. Internally the eastern dome rests on a moulded cornice with consoles and pendentives without a drum; but the western cupolas have squinches and octagonal drums. They are supported by

71. STILO (*Reggio Calabria*). *The Cattolica*

round arches on composite piers which also form the three corresponding bays of the vaulted aisles—a daring scheme of contiguous hemispherical shapes and spaces. Further south in Calabria the basilican monastery churches of Stilo and Rossano are an exotic sight. Built on a Greek-cross plan inscribed in a square, the rough brick church of Stilo over-hanging the cliffs has three round apses rising sheer from the rockface. These shapes correspond with the cylindrical domes, one in the ntcere and four smaller ones at the corners of the square. Such stark primeval buildings are a far cry from the Byzantine-Moslem palace churches which the Normans constructed in twelfth century Sicily.

The architecture of Sicily is of a composite nature, Greek and Roman, Byzantine and Saracen, Norman and Suabian. The Normans conquered the island between 1061 and 1091. The Germans united it with the Holy Roman Empire in 1194. One of its grandest monuments,

72. CEFALU (*Palermo*). *Cathedral*

73. CEFALU (*Palermo*). *Cathedral. Apse*

72 the Cathedral of Cefalù reflects these several styles. The Norman king
73 Roger II built the high apse and transept (1131-40) on a beautiful site
between a rocky escarpment and the Tyrrhenian sea. The nave was
added in 1160 and the façade in 1230 at the time of the Emperor Frederick
74 II. This Romanesque basilica with its single aisle and sober nave
reserved its Byzantine splendour to the mosaics of the cross-vaulted apse
with the seraphims above the icon of the blessing Saviour in the conch
and the Madonna Orans and two rows of apostles beneath. The narrow
apse, extended presbytery and projecting transept combined with the
unusually short nave and the fortress-like towers framing the portico and
double-arcaded façade. This monumental church was built as a mausoleum
for the Norman kings. Its height is stressed by slender coupled shafts
running up to the cornice of the apse. Though the interlaced arches
and zig zag moulding of the façade may be of Saracen origin, they have

74. Cefalu (*Palermo*). *Cathedral. Interior*

become a Norman feature. The handsome vaulted narthex between the square towers has two pointed arches flanking a round one. Cefalù Cathedral, but for its Byzantine mosaics—the finest in Sicily—and a few Moslem features, is a unified Norman building of marked individuality and poise.

Monreale Cathedral of S. Maria la Nuova is a perfect blend of the Norman Romanesque, Byzantine mosaic decoration and Moslem pointed and interlacing arches. Founded by King William II in 1174 it was already a bishopric by 1182. Monreale is a palace church and combines oriental sumptuousness with the plan of an Early Christian basilica, consisting of a wide, well lit nave, narrow aisles, antique columns supporting pointed Moslem arches with block like dosserets over Corinthian capitals. The wide transept is invisible from the nave entrance on account of its staid and regal intercolumnation. The open timber roof is brightly painted and gilded and lower than the vaulted aisles. The view along the nave culminates in the Eastern apse and choir, framed by two triumphal arches and dominated by the icon of the Pantocrator above the Virgin, archangels and apostles. Here the Roman basilica terminates in a Byzantine tripartite apse of immense height. Through its resplendent mosaics, encroaching on every available wall space, including archivolts and the areas between windows and cornice, clerestorey and colonnade, and by a great dado with inlaid marble the interior of Monreale is akin to Moslem palaces like La Cuba or La Zisa. Externally the most striking

75
(85)

76

85

G

75. MONREALE (*Palermo*). *Cathedral of S. Maria la Nuova.* *Apse*

76. MONREALE (*Palermo*). *Cathedral of S. Maria la Nuova. Interior*

view obtains from the east, where the great hemicycles of the three
apses rise up steep and solid in three storeys, ornate with blind and
interlaced arcading with disks and half-columns and broad cornices,
dark inlay in the soft yellow limestone. The west front is set between the
square cubic mass of the towers, one of them incomplete. The two
famous bronze doors are by Bonannus da Pisa and Barisanus da Trani.
Monreale clearly shows how the Norman kings welcomed the courtly
splendour of the Byzantine-Arab tradition to make the Christian basilica
more festive and to commemorate their rule.

Already prior to Monreale a wholly oriental little church had been
created inside the royal palace in Palermo: the Cappella Palatina, dedicated 77
in 1143. With three aisles and apses, a cupola on squinches, but no
transept, the royal chapel has a painted stalactite ceiling of Moorish
provenance and a sombre, gem-like profusion of mosaics covering walls
and soffits, and pointed arches with figurative and abstract design.
Byzantine and Moslem forms and decoration are of unrivalled preciousness.
The Palatine chapel is a basilica in miniature. Dimly lit but with a
radiant choir and cupola, a raised sanctuary and, in the west, a platform
for the royal court beneath a mosaic of Christ enthroned between Peter
and Paul, it is a harmonious blend of Roman, Byzantine and Islamic
culture. In the sumptuous ensemble of King Roger's chapel, stylised

87

77. PALERMO. *Palazzo dei Normanni. Capella Palatina*

78. PALERMO. *Cathedral of S. Maria Assunta*

and abstract patterns mingle freely with the haunting and expressionist icons of the Fathers of the Eastern church.

By contrast, Palermo Cathedral of S. Maria Assunta is the largest, **78** but internally least inspiring of Norman churches, reshaped in the late eighteenth century. But externally the long nave with its crenellated walls, arcaded cornices, rich mouldings and the towers and turrets at the four corners of the church, is an imposing sight where the imaginative design of the Arabs in Sicily is joined to the simple grandeur of the Normans and Hohenstaufen whose porphyry tombs are the greatest treasure of the Cathedral. Lofty spires and castellated walls and square cubic shapes are countered by diverse arabesques and wall ornaments. A fine Gothic portico with carved gable and three pointed arches on slender columns adorns the southern façade, and on the western side, the Cathedral, which was built by Archbishop Gualtieri between 1170 and 1194, is joined by a bridge to the many turretted bishop's palace.

79. PALERMO. *S. Giovanni degli Eremiti. Campanile and dome*

The Normans were great assimilators and there are in Palermo a number of pure Moslem structures. These are of compact geometrical shape, square or rectangular with hemispherical domes like mosques and **79** completely bare within. The finest is S. Giovanni degli Eremiti (*c.* 1132) with domes over the arms of the vaulted and projecting transept and a smaller one crowning the campanile. These domes rise on short cylindrical drums and vary in size and dimensions. Their swelling hemispheres, pierced by round-headed windows are clearly silhouetted **80** above the straight enclosing walls of the one-time mosque. S. Cataldo (1161) has a bare three-aisled interior with three domes on squinches and broad arches linking column to column across the nave. Externally it is even simpler than S. Giovanni, a square block of a building with **81** three identical cupolas aligned alongside the nave as in Molfetta Cathedral, but on a smaller scale. Its shape recalls one of the Palermitan pleasure palaces, a cubic block with continuous cornices and blind arcades surrounding and linking the windows in Arab fashion.

La Zisa is coeval with these Moslem churches of the Norman period in Sicily. Begun under William I in mid-twelfth century, it is a grand rectangular building whose only exterior ornaments are the in-filled arcades enframing door and window openings and two minaret-like turrets at the sides. The calm planar wall-surfaces are crenellated at roof level and their fortress-like character conceals the lavish interior of stalactite ceilings, mosaic paintings, friezes and colonettes at the corners of wall recesses. Sicilian architecture shows few signs of the

80. PALERMO. *S. Cataldo. Interior*

81. PALERMO. *S. Cataldo*

Hohenstaufen presence. Though Frederick II grew up in the royal
palace at Palermo, he left his mark mainly on the castles and figurative
sculpture of Apulia and Campania.

* * * * *

82. ROME. *Basilica of S. Paul's outside the City Walls. Cloisters*

Monastic cloisters evolved from the forecourt of basilican churches, just as the palace cortile was a secular form of the conventual cloister. One of the best preserved from the end of the twelfth century is in S. Paolo fuori (Rome). It is a most exotic sight: coffered vaulting with **82** Roman rosettes on pairs of twisted pillars or smooth ones inlaid with coloured marble and mosaics. Such work was done by the Cosmati family and by Vassaletto who designed the lovely cloister of S. Giovanni in Laterano (*c.* 1225-35). An open garden square is surrounded on all four sides by a wide groin-vaulted passage whose main supports are oblong piers with attached Ionic columns at the springing of the vault. In each bay there are four pairs of twin pillars—two smooth and two twisted—with Roman entablature and Cosmatesque frieze supporting five slender arches above a solid podium. The wall is interrupted only at the garden entrances which are flanked by seated lions.

Cosmati work of coloured marble-inlay or porphyry and gold mosaic in geometric patterns of disks, squares, stars and curvilinear or interlacing forms, often combined with sculptures, are found on pulpits, choir screen and bishop thrones, chiefly in Rome and the area around Naples. But cloisters in the decorative Moslem style were built in Amalfi as well as Monreale. The Chiostro del Paradiso adjoining the completely **84** restored Cathedral at Amalfi has interminable rows of paired colonnettes supporting sharply pointed and interlacing triple arches in the Moorish style which lend it the bewildering aspect of a linear arabesque.

83. ROME. *SS. Quattro Coronati. Cloisters (photo: E.N.I.T. Rome)*

84. AMALFI. *Cloisters of Paradise*

85. MONREALE (*Palermo*). *Cathedral cloisters*

But the monastic cloisters of Monreale Cathedral in Sicily are the most decorative of all on account of the infinite variety of imaginative forms and of views, be it across the palm-garden towards the tower or to the fountain enclosure with its tall shaft and round basin. Here too the arches are in the pointed Islamic style, but more widely spaced than in Amalfi. The twin shafts which support them are set on high undulating plinths and their double capitals are decorated with figurative sculpture of biblical and pagan themes. There are twenty-five arches on each side of the square and two hundred and sixteen columns in all, four at each corner. Arches and colonettes display an infinite wealth of ornamental motives, floral or geometrical, zigzag or lozenge patterning, fluted pillars alternating with plain, a gay, glittering splendour, holding ' the gorgeous east in fee '.

85
(75, 76)

CHAPTER THREE

GOTHIC ARCHITECTURE 1250-1400

1. CATHEDRALS AND CHURCHES OF THE NEW PREACHING ORDERS

The Italian Gothic is a style apart from its northern protagonists. There are few churches which can compare with French cathedrals or abbeys and these are of northern inspiration like Fossanova built by Cistercians from Burgundy, or Milan, perhaps the only building on Italian soil with transalpine connotations. The great Gothic cathedrals of Siena and Orvieto with their coloured marble panelling, their triangular gable, their sculptural decoration created a native form of the style, whereas their zebra banding, round arches and columns and composite piers belong to the Romanesque tradition, and are wholly different from the clustered shafts of immense height and the dissolution of walls by tall tracery windows of French cathedrals. Also in the large preaching churches of the Friars Minor belonging to the Gothic period, such as S. Croce, S. Maria Novella (Florence), the Frari and SS. Giovanni e Paolo (Venice), light, spaciousness and solid supports prevail, though Gothic attributes like pointed arch and windows and ribbed vault are adopted. Since the walls are solid, flying buttresses are dispensed with. In Italy the Gothic is tempered and modified by classical proportions, a Mediterranean sense for human scale, for breadth rather than height, averse from the transcendental aspirations of the north.

The Gothic was slow in conquering Italy. It was an alien style and rarely severed its link with the Romanesque. The northern character-istics like soaring height, dissolution of walls, flying buttresses and linear arabesques never acquired a real birthright in Italy. Gothic influences came from the French cathedrals, the Cistercians in Burgundy and via the Anjou dynasty ruling Naples. Milan cathedral was partly built by German architects, whereas Siena and Orvieto created their own distinc-tively Italianate version of the Gothic. The large hall churches of the Friars Minor which sprang up in large cities like Bologna, Florence, Siena and Venice, excelled in spaciousness, light and harmony rather than in intricate linear dynamics, the mysticism of light filtered through stained glass windows and the soaring aspirations after the supernatural.

Rome rejected the Gothic altogether, with one gloomy exception, S. Maria Sopra Minerva, built by Florentine architects. In the course of the thirteenth and fourteenth centuries great cathedrals and monastic foundations arose mainly in Tuscany and in Umbria. The evolution of city states, their growing wealth, might and ambition are reflected in their architecture. In Florence and Siena economic and military vicissitudes influenced the story of their cathedral projects, town halls and palaces. The powerful merchant guilds and banking houses provided

96

86. SIENA. *Cathedral*

the social and financial background of religious and civic buildings on a grand scale.

Simultaneous with the proud cathedrals, the religious movement which came in the wake of the Franciscan and Dominican Orders engendered a much simpler type of church, free from ornamental richness and display, serving a dual purpose, that of preaching to large crowds and of saying mass. The Italian Gothic is tempered and restrained by the Romanesque tradition, accepting certain decorative and structural innovations, but rarely the whole of the new style. In France, Germany and England cathedrals rose to immense height, with many-ribbed vaults, borne on slender shafts, and with wall-divisions of four storeys, galleries and large window spaces to effect lightness, airiness, verticality; the Italians adopted but few of these characteristics like the pointed arch or cross-rib vaulting. They preferred clarity of design to the bewildering multiplicity of parts and solid walls enclosing wide spaces with horizontal rather than vertical stresses.

86   Perhaps the finest achievement of the Italian Gothic, the façade of Siena Cathedral, is primarily a sculptural monument owing to the genius of Giovanni Pisano. It had a protracted history which strongly reflects upon its present shape. Built between 1226 and 1380, the original nave, aisles, narrow transept and vaulted cupola were completed by 1264. It was then a Romanesque basilica. By 1284 the greatest sculptor of the age, Giovanni Pisano was present in Siena, designing the lower section of the façade and its remarkable sculpture. Since 1290 he figures as architect in charge of the cathedral, but seven years later he abandoned this work and left for Pisa. In 1316 it was decided to extend the nave by two bays and in order to provide a substructure for this extension the Baptistry of S. Giovanni was built in lieu of a crypt beneath the east-end. Later the clerestorey was enlarged to heighten the nave and this entailed the raising of the façade to conceal it.

The greatest architects of the age contributed to the building of Siena Cathedral which rose in rivalry to those in Florence and Orvieto. In 1316 Lorenzo Maitani, a native of Siena and the designer of the lower section of the façade at Orvieto was put in charge and, after the Black Death of 1348 had interrupted all work for a decade, Francesco Talenti, architect of S. Maria del Fiore, was called in. Meanwhile an ambitious scheme by which the old basilica was to serve as a transept to an entirely new cathedral had to be abandoned.

87   Looking along the nave towards the choir the prevalent impression is one of unity in complexity. To this the black and white marble banding of heavy piers under the blue and gold of the ribbed cross-vaulting

87. SIENA. *Cathedral. Interior*

contributes as much as the great round-headed arches leading towards
the hexagonal crossing and the brightly lit sanctuary beyond. Here is
the climax of the cathedral with the great cupola spanning the width of

89. Orvieto. *Cathedral. Interior*

the canopy-curtain; but the Madonna and Child are of marble. Maitani's sculptures differ from Giovanni Pisano's by their northern inwardness and gaunt shape, their regal stance. Raised on a podium, Orvieto Cathedral stands on a hill beside the Palace of the Popes, a landmark of the purest Tuscan Gothic. The flanking walls of the building and the half-cylinders of the aisle-niches are marked by zebra banding throughout.

S. Peter's apart, no building in Italy holds greater sway over the imagination than the Florentine Cathedral of S. Maria del Fiore. This is due to the grandeur of Brunelleschi's cupola, dominating town and river valley, and to the unified complex of Duomo, Campanile and Baptistery. The compact marble-clad exterior in white and green beneath the red roof and cupolas, the retreating and advancing polygonal chapels at the east-end of the church, the firm seating of the octagonal drum over the crossing convey a sense of mass and weight and power, an organic whole, grown, not made; longitudinal nave and centrally orientated sanctuary are firmly knit together.

This splendid shell is in marked contrast to the uncommonly severe and puritanical interior of the Cathedral. It has a checkered history. The original plan by Arnolfo di Cambio was only partly executed. The foundation goes back to 1296 and Pope Boniface VIII. Building began in the Jubilee year of 1300. Arnolfo probably died in 1302. After an interval of 32 years Giotto and his pupil Andrea Pisano took over. The famous Campanile—Giotto's Tower—was built, rising in five tiers with

90. FLORENCE. *Cathedral of S. Maria del Fiore. Interior*

gabled tracery windows and corbelled cornice, its coloured marble panels matching the adjoining cathedral wall. In 1357 the new architect was Francesco Talenti. He increased height and width of the nave and lengthened it by a fourth bay. The crossing and the polygonal chapels surrounding it on three sides, as well as the drum, spanning a width of 140 feet, in preparation for Brunelleschi's cupola were to follow.

The simple grandeur of the spacious nave, completed in 1420, **90** resides in its plain wall surfaces and basic architectural members: massive angular piers supporting a ribbed stone vault, and a heavy cornice running all round the building including the central octagon. The altar was moved from the apse to the crossing. There are only three free-standing piers supporting four grand arches and a quadripartite vault. The great length of the nave and its classical measure, twice as high as it is wide, account for the unity of the interior space, containing the aisles as a lateral extension. Height is tempered by breadth, and Gothic verticality arrested by weighty piers with horizontal mouldings and capitals.

Movement through the nave is directed towards the centralised space under the dome from which the three apsidal tribunes radiate, each containing five chapels. The same unified complexity governs the domed and many-sided exterior. In spite of the Latin-cross plan of S. **91** Maria del Fiore, the classical aspirations of the Renaissance were to be **(136)**

103

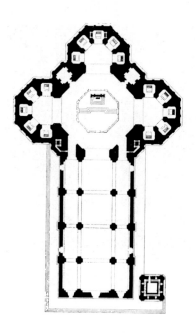

91. FLORENCE. *Cathedral of*
S. Maria dei Fiori (from Montigny)

vindicated in the next century by Brunelleschi's triumphant dome over
the octagonal crossing, gathering in the apses as well as the nave.

In monastic architecture it was the Cistercians from Burgundy who
92 introduced the early Gothic style in Italy. The abbey-church of Fossanova
south of Rome, built between 1179 and 1208 is in fact the first Gothic
monument on Italian soil. Its simple exterior consists of a long nave
and choir with aisles and projecting transepts. Choir and chapels are
rectangular. There are no flying buttresses, only applied ones supporting
the outer walls. An octagonal tower in two tiers with a lantern rises over
the crossing. Internally Fossanova is of exceptional purity. The groin-
vaulted nave has pointed arches growing out of half-columns attached to
composite piers. There are two rose windows, one over the façade,
the other in the east. The spiritual beauty of Fossanova is in ' the
mysterious harmony of numbers ' (Mâle) and in the absence of ornament,
for even the capitals are reduced to angular mouldings or stylised foliage.
93 The same sobriety prevails in the ancient cloister whose broad arches
rest upon paired columns with half capitals and plain pulvins enclosing
a wild luxuriant garden. Cistercian churches are cruciform and their
distinguishing feature, apart from flat end-walls of choir and transepts
is the great central tower over the crossing.

92. Fossanova. *Abbey church*

93. FOSSANOVA. *Abbey cloisters*

94   One of the finest is in Chiaravalle Milanese (1220), the architectural climax of a small abbey church, rising in multiple and arcaded tiers with tall windows to a cone shaped spire. French Gothic and Lombard features combine in the elaborate superstructure of the tower which dwarfs the church squatting beneath. But it was the Friars Minor who proliferated their own ingenuous type of preacher's church all over Italy which shared with the Cistercians a basic severity and simplicity of form. They adopted the ogival arch but preferred the square and detached Lombard belfry to the intricate crossing tower.

95   With the rapid growth of the Franciscan and Dominican Orders spacious hall-like churches were required. S. Francesco at Assisi set the pace; others followed in Florence, Siena, Bologna, the Veneto and elsewhere. The building of S. Francesco began in 1228 two years after the death of the saint. A crypt-like and single-naved cruciform church was hollowed out of the rock, a dark, low and cavernous vault, spanned by huge Roman arches, its five bays roofed by broad cross-ribbed vaults. **96** This lower church is a solemn and mysterious place richly decorated and **97** sparsely lit. The upper church, supported externally by cylindrical buttresses and flanked by a ponderous square tower, is wholly different. The single aisleless nave is a unified space, airy and luminous with five square bays and Gothic vaulting, where piers of clustered half-columns attached to the walls support pointed arches and scan the space. A great hall, serene and festive, its planar walls beneath the two-light windows

94.   CHIARAVALLE MILANESE.   *Abbey Church (photo: Perotti/E.P.T. Milan)*

97. ASSISI. *Basilica of S. Francesco. Upper church*

98. SIENA. *S. Domenico*

by round or Early Gothic windows. In S. Domenico the transept seems **98**
wedged into the nave, supported externally by attached buttresses of
cyclopic size.

About a century after the inception of S. Francesco at Assisi, there
rose at the southern tip of Umbria in the hill town of Todi, the birthplace of Jacopone poet of the *Stabat Mater*, the church of S. Fortunato
which is the acme of the Franciscan hall church (1292-1328). Its wide **99**
and square frontage is reached by steps and entered by a large roundheaded
porch with minor ones on either side. The vastness of its interior space **100**
is based on classical proportions—the nave being twice as wide as the
aisles—the soaring height of clustered piers on stout bases, continuing
above the capitals before fanning out like palm-leaves into the shapely
rib vaulting. The triumphant apse has seven sides and the four large
bays leading towards it are spaced so well that the view across the church is
nowhere impeded. Indeed the aisles do not interrupt the airy unity of
the enclosed space with its bare walls articulated only by six side chapels
and blind arches above. A pulpit is stuck high on the wall of the right
aisle and this is open to the diagonal view from the main body of the
church. The only obstruction—a functional necessity—are the tie-
beams of solid masonry linking nave piers with aisle pilasters to act as

99. TODI. *S. Fortunato*

interior buttresses, holding together outer walls and vault-supporting pillars.

S. Fortunato exemplifies the mature style of a Franciscan basilica with its dual purpose of preaching and saying mass, by the airy vastness of its main body and the proliferation of open chapels and altars. Its elegance results from the generous proportions, its uncommon height, unadorned walls, vast bays and slim composite pillars formed by eight half-columns, its light and lightness and multiple views. It is a felicitous blend of Gothic elements with the Umbrian Romanesque.

The chief Dominican church in Florence is S. Maria Novella (begun in 1279), with ribbed vault in dark pietra serena and wide span of arches between slender piers composed of half columns. S. Maria Novella contrasts with the northern Gothic by its spaciousness, airiness, lightness. The width of square bays, the narrow aisles and limited height favour a feeling of unity, of free movement and unimpeded vistas towards the pulpit as well as the sanctuary with its contracted space, rectangular

100. TODI. *S. Fortunato. Interior*

apse and triple windows. Projecting transept and four square chapels, flanking the apse, complete the cruciform plan of the church whose nave and aisles intermingle harmoniously and where the engaged columns have carved capitals in the classical tradition.

101
(140)
But the greatest Florentine church of the mendicant orders is S. Croce built by the Franciscans in rivalry with the Dominican S. Maria Novella. It was probably planned by Arnolfo di Cambio between 1294 and 1301, with a five-sided apse, as in the upper church of Assisi, but almost wholly pierced by the tall lancet windows and framed by the great pointed arch at the crossing. The aisles are joined to the nave by slender piers, supporting a limited expanse of wall and a timber roof, instead of a heavy rib-vaulting. Seven wide bays enhance the airiness of the unified space.

The great length and breadth of S. Croce, syncopated by beams of the open truss roof and the sharply defined arcade culminate in the tall triumphal arch, pierced by four minor arches, framing the light-filled apse. Five lofty chapels on either side of the apse are decorated in the light pastel tints of Giotto's and Gaddi's frescoes. These chapels, endowed by the new plutocracy of Florence—the Bardi, Peruzzi and Baroncelli—are arranged in one row, they do not radiate in a wide circle as in S. Francesco, Bologna and are terminated by flat end walls.

S. Croce is the apogee of Italian Gothic where verticality of apse and entrance arch and pointed windows is balanced by the flat roof and the vast space humanized by noble proportion. For ultimately the

102. PISA. *S. Maria della Spina*

aesthetic appeal depends on the architectural module, the height and diameter of piers or columns, and the distance between them which determines the shape of the bays. At S. Croce the wide nave and narrow aisles and the great horizontal string course counteract the Gothic elements creating a sense of spaciousness and repose.

The quintessence of the Tuscan Gothic is to be found in small oratories like S. Maria della Spina at Pisa (*c.* 1323). But the florid **102** ornamentation does not conceal the disciplined build-up of basic forms, especially in the façade where two wide arches, framed by buttresses, spanning the whole width, are surmounted by crocketed gables and, for good measure, a third one, set back in the centre over the central tabernacle. Two rose windows, plumb over the doorways, and a crown of five more tabernacles enshrining figures complete the exhilarating design where delicate pointed and corbelled shapes are held in balance by depressed arches and projecting cornices. A wealth of decoration is deployed on the side walls where a filigree of twelve gabled tabernacles on slender shafts harbouring sculptures is wedged between six higher and turreted structures. But on ground floor level round arches contain the Gothic

103. FLORENCE. *Loggia of the Bigallo*

104. PADUA. *Basilica of S. Antonio (Il Santo)*

windows, and an overhanging cornice serves as a stark horizontal base for the sculptural articulations above, conceived as architecture on a miniature scale. Thus even the purest example of the florid Gothic in Tuscany is restrained by Romanesque elements and only the continuous gallery of tabernacles at the sides conceals the basically simple form of the church enclosing the plain interior space with decorative profusion. The exterior of S. Maria della Spina is predominantly Gothic with simple interior divisions.

The Florentine Or San Michele, once a cornmarket, then in 1337 transformed into a church, is a precious casket within, and has a sober exterior containing deep niches for full-length sculptures. But the Gothic richness of painted and carved ornament and Orcagna's florid tabernacle do not conceal the Romanesque structure, the square bays and massive piers supporting round arches and broad rib-vaulting. The cusped gables, finials and figurines, the painted pilasters and archivolts belong to the international style, but the grand arches over rectangular spatial units, the polygonal supports with acanthus leaf capitals buttressing the wide span of the vault are of the medieval world of the Romanesque.

Like Or San Michele the Loggia del Bigallo (1352-81), a shelter for **103** foundlings, combines architectural with ornamental and even pictorial

I

105. VENICE. *SS. Giovanni e Paolo*

effects. Round arches, enclosed within rectangles, and square piers set on high podiums are carved in low relief: arabesques, rosettes, spiral columns, beside pierced roundels and tabernacles. These lighten but do not conceal the firm structural frame, and the Bigallo with its finely wrought gate testifies to the Florentine fusion of basically Romanesque forms with stylish Gothic ornamentation.

Vast Franciscan and Dominican churches rose during the thirteenth and fourteenth centuries also in Venice and the Venetian hinterland, amongst them the pilgrimage church of S. Antonio, in Padua. This proclaimed its vicinity to S. Marco by a succession of seven domes on high cylindrical drums over nave, transepts and choir. S. Antonio (*Il Santo*) (1231-1307) presents a veritable fusion of styles, Byzantine, Romanesque and Gothic, also in the interior with its nine chapels surrounding the apse, its ambulatory and rough bare walls, the coexistence of round arches and pointed windows. Externally the Lombard Romanesque geometry of a square and gabled façade with an arcaded gallery blends uneasily with the polygonal towers and many shaped domes. The dim interior, an enclosed space on a grandiose scale, is redeemed chiefly by Donatello's High Altar reliefs and free standing sculpture. S. Antonio remained without succession, a syncretistic monument, awesome, ungainly, overpowering, expression of 'gigantic forces locked in ponderous battle '.

104

106. VENICE. *S. Maria Gloriosa dei Frari*

Venice too had her main churches of the Franciscan and Dominican observance: SS. Giovanni e Paolo and the Frari. The former is the **105** Westminster of the Doges; it is also the paradigma of the Venetian Gothic, begun in 1333 with four chapels flanking the polygonal apse, almost wholly pierced by tracery windows in two tiers with oculi intervening. Narrow aisles accompany the lofty nave, where fully round stone columns, linked by wood beams, reach up to the ribbed vault by flat pilaster strips. Externally, attached buttresses stress the verticality of the walls, broken into by triple windows. A dome over the crossing seems a concession to Byzantine Venice; the façade is indebted to the Romanesque Lombard tradition of brick and stone masonry.

S. Maria Gloriosa dei Frari has six eastern transept chapels and **106** massive stone columns, similarly tied to the outer walls across nave and aisles. But the vaults are lower and wider and a sense of weight and of breadth keeps check on Gothic upward trends. Externally the polygonal end walls of apses and transepts present a succession of vertical planes alternating with long recessed windows. In the high luminous space of S.S. Giovanni e Paolo the cylindrical columns are in no conflict with the pointed arches and tall tracery windows. But the Frari church is darker and heavier, a broad avenue of mighty piers, cut short by a choir screen before the crossing, under a lower vault, mysteriously lit from the sides and main apse.

The fame of S. Petronio, Bologna, is based on its great size and **107** harmonious divisions, rivalling the cathedrals of Milan and Florence,

107. BOLOGNA. *Basilica of S. Petronio*

and on Jacopo della Quercia's relief sculpture around the central doorway of its stepped façade. Designed by Antonio di Vincenzo in 1390, S. Petronio was conceived on too vast a scale to present a natural habitat. Only nave and aisles and flanking chapels were ever completed but without the elaborately planned east end and ambulatory. Its six square bays, measuring sixty-three feet, between well spaced compound piers—attached pilasters and half columns with mouldings in place of capitals as in Florence—and their lateral extensions account for the great width of the church. The long vista of the nave presents an unbroken sequence of arcading and pointed vaults with round windows set high into the planar walls.

The flat surfaces on piers, soffits and choir arch blend with the rounded shapes and no horizontal cornice disturbs the impression of height and the rhythmical progression of bays and vaults. By the soaring slenderness of the shafts from which the steeply pointed ribs and transversal arches spring, S. Petronio redeems its uncommon vastness—a significant work of the Late Gothic in Italy, monumental without heaviness, spacious, serene and lucid, without the shaded mysteries of the northern Gothic.

108

108. *Bologna. Basilica of S. Petronio. Interior*

In S. Petronio the great length and height of the nave presents a final Gothic solution, culminating in the elegant pointed rib vaulting of the apse sprung from corbels. Other than Milan with its northern gloom and solemnity, S. Petronio's light-filled vastness and Lombard façade masking the interior is an indigenous Italian form of the Gothic where solid supports and soaring structures are in perfect equipoise. In Italy ribbed vaults were adopted, but flying buttresses proved unnecessary, for the side walls were unbroken by stained glass windows and not in need of external supports. The Italians, wrote Emile Male, considered solid walls as ' an object of beauty '. They liked to construct ever larger churches with wide arcading and classical proportions. Their emphasis was on breadth rather than height, on spaciousness, coolness, light and air.

Only Milan Cathedral is a true example of the northern Gothic in **109** Italy. It is the epitome of the Late Gothic style. With S. Petronio, Bologna, it is also the largest in width as well as in height of Italian churches and its most northern in form as in spirit. Built between 1385 and 1485 by Italian, French and German architects and situated at the gateway to the south, Milan Cathedral was begun by Giovanni Galeazzo Visconti and largely completed under Lodovico Sforza. It has four aisles, a double transept, polygonal choir, ambulatory and domical vault. Its finest features are the tall tracery windows and the forest of lofty piers with engaged half-columns and capitals so large as to contain canopied figure sculptures all round. The pointed arches of the nave are accompanied by steeply vaulted aisles. There are no side chapels, no triforium

gallery. But the very height and number of multiple piers, the small clerestorey, the steepness of cross-ribbed vaulting, the muted rainbow colours of the tracery windows with their delicate interlacing pattern and the vast perspective views lend to Milan Cathedral the hushed and solemn mood of the northern Gothic.

Such dark and awe-inspiring forest vastness is strangely matched by the glittering white marble finery of the exterior, the excessive ornateness and dissolution of solid walls, the flying buttresses, the pinnacles crowned with statues, the wealth of intricate lace work in stone surrounding the tall slim tracery-windows of the aisles or the three larger ones of the apse. Yet with all its richness and complexity Milan Cathedral has an inbuilt geometrical order and proportion. It has been argued that the Lombard architects modified the High Gothic influence from beyond the Alps by disallowing a steeply pitched roof or aisles of equal height with the nave. Yet the overall impression of the dimly lit interior is its kinship with the hushed and mystical mood of northern cathedrals, the towering height and relentless succession of piers and Gothic vaults engendering movement towards the altar and the ' evocative half light ' from stained glass windows.

In a sense Milan is the only Gothic cathedral in Italy and in the context of Lombard architecture the most disingenuous. Its finest and oldest part is the apsidal exterior with the interlacing linearism of the great windows, the fretwork of stone, the elegant spires. Drum and cupola are work of the sixteenth century (Amadeo) and the wide façade is of the nineteenth. The great pile of the building with its marble-clad roof supports an infinite number of arrow-like motifs piercing the sky. Built on a colossal scale and firmly placed on a heavy base the cathedral lies in eternal strife with its exuberant, restless and multiform vertical members.

CHAPTER THREE

GOTHIC ARCHITECTURE 1250-1400

2. FORTIFIED BUILDINGS AND CIVIC PALACES

Italian castles from the Middle Ages to the Renaissance seek to combine the requirements of a stronghold with aesthetic qualities. From the Staufen Emperor Frederick's castles to Francesco di Giorgio's military architecture the oneness and shapeliness of geometrical bodies—cube, cone or sphere—determine structures. Curtain walls, strengthened by prismatic towers at regular intervals abound. Siting is at strategic points on some eminence or protected by lake or river. Often a division between the castle and a walled forecourt for the soldiers' quarters is made. Or else a forbidding fortress is built at the city's edge by the local tyrant with state and living rooms as well as barracks, moat and dungeon, keep, drawbridge and embattled walls. Besides the castles and tower houses of the factious city-communes and ruling families of northern and central Italy, town halls and civic buildings also stressed the defensive aspect. Although smaller townships developed a simple oblong structure with an open arcade on ground level and a council chamber in the upper storey, the larger cities especially in Tuscany and in Umbria, built public palaces of militant solidity, square blocks with few windows, crenellated roofs and threatening towers, lofty symbols of civic pride. Among these Palazzo Vecchio at Florence and Palazzo Pubblico at Siena are the most conspicuous. But the hill towns of Umbria like Todi or Gubbio, sited their fortified seats of government as an integral part of a planned town centre. The Doge's Palace at Venice stands apart as a monument of the Veneto-Byzantine Gothic, architectural pagantry based on fabulous riches and an aristocratic society.

Castles, towers, town walls and fortified houses proliferated in Italy between the early middle ages and the Renaissance. Their origin is the Roman wall encircling, sheltering towns and citizens. The Norman keep is a significant feature as is the long curtain-wall, punctuated by towers at regular intervals or the formidable bastion of the overlords of the city-states, the Visconti, Scaligeri, Este, Gonzaga. Powerful feudal families built towers or tower-houses and the first palaces of the Renaissance were strongholds for defence and refuge as well as city dwellings. But the medieval castles which the Emperor Frederick II built mainly in southern Italy, but also at Prato are distinguished by their functional shape, their strength, judicious siting and aesthetic qualities. Of these Castle del Monte in the Basilicata is the best preserved and the most impressive. Frederick II grew up in Sicily and assimilated Eastern and Western civilisations, Roman, Norman and Arabic. His body-guard was Saracen. His life's struggle was with the Papacy, and with the cities cleft between Guelf and Ghibelline factions, to establish the Imperial rights over Italy.

Castle del Monte overlooking a wide panorama of land and seashore 110
was built about 1240 on an octagonal plan: an inner court, an outer wall
and eight angle towers.   It had eight rooms on two storeys and a Gothic
porch with classical trabeation.   The façade with its double stairway
leading to the entrance platform, the pilasters with acanthus leaf capitals
supporting a carved architrave and pediment enclosed by a rectangle,
the central window repeating the pointed shape of the portal and the tall
and narrow niches at the sides with the extended tower cornice for a
base contribute to a design of great dignity.   Castel del Monte might
have served as a hunting lodge for falconry, the emperor's favourite
pastime, a retreat for pleasure rather than war.   Its geometrical form with
the prismatic bodies of projecting towers, only slightly higher than the
short connecting walls is of singular oneness and harmony.   The faintly
pointed shape of the windows is Arab or early Gothic, one between each
pair of towers.   There are larger windows in the eight inter-connected
rooms overlooking the inner court.   The emperor's state room was on
the eastern side, above the portal, overlooking the sea, and here the
architectural ornament blends classical and Gothic forms in perfect
harmony.   Viewed from a distance, Castel del Monte is a stark formalized
structure, a centrally planned regular body of compact symmetry, grown
not made, with its alternating rhythm of hexagonal tower facets and walls,
of articulate mass and masonry.   Its beauty lies in a synthesis of cubic

111. PRATO. *Castello dell'Imperatore*

solids and planar surfaces within the basic pattern of the closed octagonal space.

Frederick's castles were concentrated in Sicily, Apulia and Catania, whence to defend his heritage and to hold sway over the cities of the papal states. They combine Gothic and Arab motifs like Castel Ursino, and their stylish regularity of impenetrable walls surrounding a square compound is punctuated by cylindrical or angular towers projecting outwards and marked at the four corners by greater height and volume.

111 In the late 1240s Frederick built Prato Castle of bright unfaced stone. It is a monumental structure by its shapely sequence of square and polygonal towers, broad and squat, projecting from the recessed walls in short intervals of space, crenellated and of equal height— a compact mass of geometrical bodies with sharp facets. It is a basic shape in the functional and aesthetic sense, a prototype from which all subsequent military architecture depends, even to the fortified mansions of the Este and Gonzaga in Mantua and Ferrara at the end of the fourteenth century.

Curtain walls punctuated by towers at regular intervals surrounding a hill town provided the basic form for medieval fortifications placed at
112 strategic points. Thus the walls of Monteriggione with its fourteen square towers, built before 1220 by the city of Siena as an outpost against the encroaching power of Florence, was so impressive that Dante made visual reference to it in the *Inferno* . . .

> Come in sù la cerchia tonda
> Montereggion di torre si corona . . .

Monteriggione on its height is crowned by a full circle of towers, he wrote in the thirty-first canto.

126

112. MONTERIGGIONI (*Siena*). *Castle*

By contrast the Castle at Sirmione, built for the Scaligeri dynasty **113** of Verona towards the end of the thirteenth century, is totally different in shape and purpose. Not raised on an eminence, but at the water's edge at the southern tip of Lake Garda, protecting the Lombard plain and itself protected by the natural moat of lake and asymmetrical harbour, Sirmione Castle circumscribes an oblong space by long crenellated curtain walls with stout bastions at the four corners. The keep rises high in splendid isolation on the lake side of the courtyard, and the large defensive complex of extended walls, watchtowers, breakwaters, draw-bridges and fortified gates is an ingenious military outpost rather than a residence like Frederick's castle with its small-scale cross-vaulted living rooms. Yet the redoubtable nature of Sirmione's defences does not impinge upon the sheer beauty of its ' landscape architecture ', its seem-ingly low embattled walls enclosing a regular well proportioned space and stretching far into the dreaming lake. Castles developed from the purely military purpose to fortified dwellings of magnificence and power. Sirmione was a defensive structure; its beauty lies in its siting and un-cluttered appearance.

Fenis Castle in the Val d'Aosta is at the opposite pole. Built on an **114** eminence, small in scale and irregular in plan, it stands on three levels with a tangle of towers of varying size and shape, cylindrical or square, with small windows at the top. The inner stronghold, surrounding an asymmetrical court is ringed at short intervals by two castellated walls decreasing in height. This compressed pile of buildings, an inner castle concealing a maze of small rooms and the closely set guard-towers of low meandering curtain walls without, appears romantic rather than formidable.

113. SIRMIONE. *Rocca Scaligera*

114. FENIS (*Aosta*). *The Castle*

115. SPOLETO. *View of the Rocca and the Ponte delle Torri*

During the second half of the fourteenth century many a *rocca* dominating Umbrian hill towns like Assisi or Spoleto were built on a regular plan, firmly and broadly esconced on a terraced plateau, commanding town and surrounding country. Such castles lay sphinx-like and threatening on the brow of the hill. At Spoleto a Roman aqueduct with high Gothic arches bridging the valley is the only link between town and fortress. The latter a long horizontal structure conjoins two rectangular spaces, a four-towered castle and a lower walled-in forecourt with two frontal keeps composing its stepped up silhouette. The forecourt served as barracks and the castle proper with its sheer unadorned walls is an early example of the fortified palace such as Bartolino da Novara was to build on a grander scale in Mantua and Ferrara. 115

These were no longer on a hillside, but at the edge of a town, surrounded by a moat or bounded by a lake. At Ferrara the palace and its main walls are strengthened at the four corners by huge square towers, fearsome cubic structures with ramps and machicolations, dwarfing the surrounding city, an expression of the ruler's might. Stylistically the castle presents a sequence of advancing and retreating planes and razor-sharp edges with square auxiliary buildings squatting in front of them. Such castles were designed to strike fear into the heart of the people, with ample provision for soldiery, armour, dungeons, but also for state and living rooms of a city palace. At Mantua, built on a similar square and compact plan, the Gonzaga eventually transformed the forbidding fortress into a house of gracious living, chiefly by dint of Mantegna's bright and audacious murals in the Camera degli Sposi and by kindred decorations of numerous small rooms, stairways and a Renaissance cortile. 116

A quite different palace cum castle was built by the Visconti at Pavia. Conceived on a very large scale, it has to all intents and purposes, 117

116. FERRARA. *Castello Estense*

117. PAVIA. *Visconti Castle*

118. SAN GIMIGNANO. *View showing towers*

become a sumptuous town residence with a spacious arcaded courtyard whose crenellated walls blend strangely with the four-part Gothic windows above the long and graceful arcade with wide arches on sturdy columns. Disks and roundels and trefoil openings within the semicircular arches of the first floor enhance the lightness of the inner court, whereas the castellated façade of equal length, flanked by two war-like towers, has rows of two-light windows on both storeys. Except for the massive corner towers and the tooth-like embattlements, the Visconti castle is a noble palace building, distinguished in the interior courtyard by a classical feeling for order, measure and symmetry.

Towers were built during the middle-ages not only as campanili but to serve the ruling families as fortified dwelling places in the factious townships of Italy. The most conspicuous example even today is the Tuscan hill town of San Gimignano where thirteen square prismatic structures straddle the serried rows of houses with warlike and menacing forms, few window-openings and hardly an ornament. Towers appear at regular distances upon city walls, sheer, rock-like and unadorned, mute reminders of danger threatening from avid neighbours. Towers were also status symbols of the aristocracy built as refuge and defence in internecine strife. Hundreds of them marked the skyline of Florence and Bologna and in the latter city the stark leaning towers Asinelli and Garisenda, built during the early twelfth century, are still a significant landmark. During the Gothic period towers on townhalls and seats of government were an expression of civic might and defiance, lofty and slim with crenellated crown like Torre del Mangia of Siena's Palazzo Pubblico or that of Palazzo Vecchio in Florence. Tower houses were not only the

118

119

119. BOLOGNA. *The Asinelli and Garisenda towers*

privilege of the ruling families and feudal factions of medieval communes; their public buildings offered the same warlike aspect, were in fact undisguised fortresses.

Small civic buildings in medieval Italy followed a common pattern: a large council chamber built over an open arcade, and a watch tower at one end. They were called *broletto* on account of the surrounding meadow where the people foregathered, or *arengario* after the small balcony or external pulpit from which they could be harangued. Such buildings still exist in many a small town like Monza, Como or Brescia.

120. COMO. *Torre Comunale and Broletto*

At Volterra or Florence the open arcade was replaced by a solid basement for defence with few windows—sometimes with an arcaded inner court-yard—and the town hall assumed a fortress-like aspect. The Broletto at Como of about 1200 is the prototype of the medieval town hall, a rectangular one-storeyed block whose wide Romanesque arches rest firmly and squarely on short octagonal piers. The building is linked to the cathedral on one side and terminated by a tower of rusticated stone on the other. Bands of coloured marble, red, grey and white, vary the wall surfaces, as do the arcaded cornices, the three-light windows and long balcony (arengario) facing the piazza. In spite of the recessed Gothic windows with their multiple shafts, the style of the Broletto is Romanesque,

120

K

121. FLORENCE. *Palazzo del Podestà (Bargello)*

for even the windows are enclosed by round arches and the horizontal mouldings and low upper storey increase the impression of weight and thrust.

Crenellated summits, sparing window openings, high steeples and other defensive superstructures were common to the Bargello and

122. FLORENCE. *Bargello. Courtyard*

the Palazzo Vecchio in Florence. The former, seat of the Podestà,   121
was founded in 1255 rising sheer in three storeys, divided by horizontal
string courses, a geometrical body of a building with two-light windows
in the first storey and a large central one in the Sala del Consiglio.
Rusticated stone, embattled roof and the unmitigated solid of the upper
storey contribute to the uncompromising severity of the Bargello. But,
like other palaces of the great, it has a fine spacious courtyard with down-
stair arcading and first floor loggia. These do not correspond; for the   122

123. FLORENCE. *Palazzo Vecchio (Palazzo della Signoria)*

portico has a wide elliptical span of arches and octagonal piers supporting a vaulted passage, whereas the upper loggia divides into many small and circular arches; an open air staircase below and a well in the centre make the cortile of the Bargello one of the most attractive in Florence.

123   Palazzo Vecchio was started in 1299 on a grander and more sophisticated scale than the Bargello whose storeys are all equal in height whereas those of the Signoria diminish at the top. There is an elaborate and aggressive superstructure, a large fortified overhang in three parts:

124. FLORENCE. *Palazzo Vecchio. Courtyard and fountain*

machicolations, dark openings and crenellation. The volume of the 124
building has sharp linear definitions of planes, articulated by two rows 125
of narrow windows topped by voussoir arches, and the great tower is
firmly seated off-centre. The overhang of the main block is repeated
on the tower above, the plain prism of the shaft, elegantly proportioned
symbol of the militant communal spirit.

137

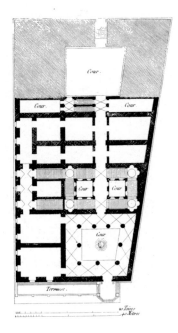

125. FLORENCE. *Palazzo Vecchio*
(*from Montigny*)

126 Robustness and austerity of the Palazzo Vecchio contrast and blend with the Loggia dei Lanzi (1376-81). The wide yet lofty Romanesque arches on strong compound piers beneath the horizontal masonry and ornamental cornice reach only to the second storey of the Signoria. Together they determine the urbanistic aspect of the piazza where the open arcades of a cross-vaulted, proto-Renaissance hall, used for ceremonial occasions, and a square medieval palace complement each other in a notable synthesis of voids and solids.

127 In mid-fourteenth century, public and private buildings shared the external severity of a fortified dwelling. Palazzo Davanzati in Florence stands out by its tall and narrow frontage, a high base with three depressed arches and identical storeys following with five windows each. The palace was crowned by embattlements, later replaced by a handsome loggia and overhanging roof. The masonry is finely graded from voussoir arches and rustication below to the smooth stonework in the upper reaches of the wall. Regularity, symmetry and strength are the hallmark of this palace-fortress which had also a small inner court with a steep stairway giving access to the richly carved and frescoed rooms. Inside and out Palazzo Davanzati bespeaks an intense and dramatic way of life.

138

126. FLORENCE. *Loggia dei Lanzi* (*photo: E.P.T. Florence*)

Roughly contemporaneous with Palazzo Vecchio is the more graceful and Gothicising Town Hall of Siena, built between 1288 and 1310, its frontis-piece wings extended by a third storey during the seventeenth century. Forming the lower boundary of the incomparable city square or Campo which is like a great shell-formed amphitheatre, Palazzo Pubblico differs from the Florentine seats of government by its apparent lightness and elegance, more palace than fortress. Its low long frontage with two rows of loggias and three-light windows and the immensely slim and lofty tower, its crown designed by Lippo Memmi, compose an ensemble which is linear as well as painterly, with its red brick, white marble and grey stone. Its windows are topped by in-filled pointed arches, a characteristic of Sienese palaces. This type of blind ogival arch recurs above the depressed round openings of the ground floor loggias, so that the extensive and slightly concave façade of the palace, circling the campo, is essentially Gothic in spite of its stressed horizontal. For this is countered by the embattled and turreted central section and, above all, by the resilient Torre del Mangia. Tower and turrets are to the palazzo what spire and finials are to a Gothic church, ensuring a surging vertical tendency which is unimpeded by the thin metallic cornices, mouldings and brackets. Though originally a tower-house with its broad central core containing the Sala del Gran Consiglio, the town hall is linear, ' calligraphic ' and ornamental in the Sienese tradition, in contrast to the three-dimensional

127. FLORENCE. *Davanzati Palace*

128. ORVIETO. *Palazzo del Capitano*

mass and bulk of other civic buildings in Tuscany and Umbria such as Volterra, Perugia and Orvieto. In its ' arresting skyline ' and silhouette and the painterly treatment of architectural parts the Palazzo Pubblico unites delicacy with strength.

Not only in Florence and Siena, but in many smaller provincial centres and medieval townships of central Italy public buildings of the thirteenth and fourteenth centuries formed a beautiful city centre surrounding an open square by the side of the cathedral. These were sturdy Romanesque palaces, simple blocks, adorned with some Gothic detail. One of the most arresting is in southern Umbria: the Palazzo del Capitano **128** in Orvieto of about 1280. It is a simple oblong shape enclosing the hall of the Gran Consiglio which the architect built over an open arcade which was later filled in. The form of the Roman arches recurs in the first floor as a continuous frame over the Gothic three-light windows with pierced tympana. The imaginative architect enlivened the exterior by three new elements: the double cornice enframing the windows, the great zigzagging staircase leading to a terrace above the arcade and the recessed, wave-like supports of this terrace repeating the undulations of

141

129. Todi. *Piazza del Popolo*

the cornice. The strange shape of the campanile is yet another innovation in a palace whose cubic regularity is animated by curvilinear and diagonal features, the abruptly terminated terrace, and by the warm golden tones of the local tufa stone.

Subtly varying lines of cornices, bold stairways linking palaces and extended views through Romanesque arches also distinguish the palaces in the Umbrian hill town of Todi. Here the broader and lower Palazzo del Capitano and its wide Roman arches and massive piers is joined by a long open stairway to the tall, narrow-breasted Palazzo del Popolo, crenellated, defiant, with large areas of blank walling and sparing window openings. There are altogether three palaces which form with the cathedral one of the most picturesque squares of the late middle-ages. **129** The wide piazza is flanked on one side by the Palazzo dei Priori (*c.* 1213), simple, austere with angular tower and oblong castellated body. At right angles to it and coeval is the lofty and gaunt Palazzo del Popolo with narrow three-light windows and, next to it the Palazzo del Capitano of about 1290, set back in space, ornate and harmonious, with delicate trefoil windows beneath triangular mouldings, softening the impact of the dark arched cavities below. But most striking is the bold diagonal of the ascending stairway, filling the space in front of the recessed palace and linking it to its sharply projecting neighbour. Thus the balance and spatial unity of contrasting shapes is restored and a homogenous whole created in Todi.

142

130. PERUGIA. *Palazzo del Comune* (*photo: R.I.B.A. Collection*)

In provincial capitals like Perugia the Palazzo del Comune, built **130** at the end of the thirteenth century and later extended, assumed gigantic proportions. With the Fontana Maggiore by Nicola Pisano in front of it, the palace is one of the most majestic sights in central Italy. Its great planar mass dominates the square, syncopated by long rows of trefoil windows in two storeys with cusped pointed arches and continuous cornices framing a great bare wall-space between them. Though the building is very tall, the horizontality is stressed by this bare middle section and by the repetitive rhythm of the Gothic windows. The façade is enhanced by the ' fan-like ' staircase leading to the pointed entrance arch and arcaded balcony. The embattled roof is now a mere ornament like the stone tracery of white and red marble upon grey travertine or the variety of shapes in the Gothic apertures and their ordered symmetry, lending to the massive building movement and anima- tion. As the florid Gothic develops, so the late medieval contrast met at Orvieto and Todi, between Romanesque arches and Gothic windows and the fortress-character of public buildings gives way to harmonious expressions of self-confidence, wealth and power.

131. GUBBIO. *Palazzo dei Consoli* (*photo: Gavirati/Azienda Autonoma Soggiorno e Turismo, Gubbio*)

131
The Palazzo dei Consoli in nearby Gubbio, built after 1300 by Gattapone and Angelo da Orvieto, is a prime example of the Umbrian architects' technical skill and sense of style. The task was formidable, for palace and piazza had to be carved out of a rocky escarpment close to the hills, and the palace rises upon a substructure of tall narrow arches with a diagonal ramp leading to the square and the symmetrical façade. The flank of the palace terminates in an open loggia with twin arches beneath the embattled roof, commanding a grand view over the Umbrian countryside. The face of the palazzo is level and regular and strong with Romanesque forms throughout. Two thirds of the frontage surges up sheer, reinforced by attached buttresses which evenly divide the space,

132. VENICE. *Ducal Palace*

rising to the three pairs of upper windows. A semicircular stairway of
later date leads via a rectangular section and small terrace to the central
porch by Matteo di Giovanello (Gattapone) with recessed arches and
clustered colonettes. The Palazzo dei Consoli in the solitary hill town
of Gubbio is a commanding structure, tall, and boldly defiant, extracted
from uncompromising rockface and without peers among the civic
buildings of Umbria.

It is a far cry from the fortified palace or town hall, the medieval
broletto of central and northern Italy to the flamboyantly Gothic
Doge's Palace in Venice. And yet, a basic connection exists between 132
the small palazzi communali and the spectacular climax of the Gothic
style in Italy which is the seat of the oligarchic government of the Serenis-
sima. They share the open arcade at ground level, carrying the solid
masonry of the upper storey. Only in Venice all traces of the round
arched Romanesque have disappeared and the loggias assume a lace-like
delicacy and colouristic refinement which are absent from the sturdier
and more militant monuments elsewhere. The wealth of Venice and
its Byzantine luxuriance account for this transformation of the Gothic
and its supreme achievement which is Palazzo Ducale.

133. VENICE. *Ducal Palace. Courtyard*

Its construction on medieval foundations was ordered in 1340 and after a break in the building during the years following the plague of 1348, the section containing the Sala del Gran Consiglio, between the Piazzetta and Riva degli Schiavoni, was completed by 1365. The extension towards the Cathedral of San Marco was undertaken in the same style between 1424 and 1438, whereas the great Cortile and Scala dei Giganti belong to the Renaissance. The reason for the universal fame of the Palazzo Ducale is in its luminous and silvery surface splendour and in the contrast between the cavernous darkness within the double loggias and the brightness of interlacing arches and their quatrefoil pattern within a circle. Moreover, it is an astonishing structural solution. Wall masses are normally carried on heavy piers, but here the fragile fretwork of continuous arches, balconies, ogee apertures and their airy quadrilobes are made to support a sheer wall with comparitively few openings, without offence to our logical or aesthetic sensibility. This is brought about by the exhilarating colour and design of the wall itself, a diagonal diamond pattern in rose and white, and by the crowning pinnacles which enliven the long horizontal skyline of the palace. Mass and weight of the upper storey and the oblong cubic shape, composed of its two near-identical wings—one facing the Library, the other the waterfront of the Bacino— blend harmoniously with the loggias. The coloured tapestry of the upper wall does not seem to exert weight or pressure on the filigree forms of the lower zone; they form a well proportioned and organic whole.

133
134

134. VENICE. *Ducal Palace. Scale dei Giganti*

A precedent for a double loggia was perhaps that of the Palazzo della Ragione in nearby Padua, built in 1305, a town hall of enormous length with an extensive row of depressed arches carried on very light columns. The interior is one vast empty space resembling a ship, but the decorative elements, balusters, pinnacles, oculi are no match for the Doge's palace with its rich relief sculpture of windows and capitals and the *fioritura* of the roof cornice which mellows the stark linearism of the block and melts into the soft atmosphere of the lagoon city. Perhaps in no other building of the Gothic style is the impression of repose and equilibrium attained by contrasting voids with solids, darkness with colour and light, and the most sophisticated stone carving with the unified wall space.

135

135. PADUA. *Palazzo della Ragione*

Palazzo Ducale is the culmination of the Venetian Gothic; but the
133 courtyard, begun in 1483 by Verona-born Antonio Rizzo and decorated by
Pietro Lombardo (1498) belongs to the Renaissance. Round arches
topped by roundels at ground level and pointed ones in the upper loggia
are thoroughly Venetian in their painterly effect of chiaroscuro—a quite
prelude to the ornamental middle-section which breaks with festive
splendour the even rhythm of the arcading. Here long horizontal friezes
with classical motifs and garlands intervene between the storeys. Single
and double piers with panelled reliefs alternate and the windows have
segmented tympana. In front of this richly varied façade is the Scala
dei Giganti or ceremonial staircase on the top of which the Doges were
134 crowned.

CHAPTER FOUR

EARLY RENAISSANCE ARCHITECTURE 1400-1500

Renaissance art divides into three stylistic phases: Early and High Renaissance and Mannerism. In architecture the protagonists of the first Renaissance are Filippo Brunelleschi and Leon Battista Alberti. Renaissance implies a re-birth or ' re-growth ', the appearance around 1400 of a new life-force which stimulated the study of antique art and letters and in architecture the re-discovery of classical forms. Quattrocento architecture, especially in Florence, rejecting Gothic shapes and ornaments, employs and modifies the classical orders, proportions, harmonies. Brunelleschi's Foundling Hospital establishes a new canon of grace and elegance in his spacing of fragile round arches and Corinthian colonettes, crystalline forms which recur in Angelico's or Lippi's Annunciation pictures. Brunelleschi's cupola of Florence Cathedral, a masterly feat of engineering, owes little to the Roman Pantheon, being elongated rather than hemispherical. But in churches like S. Spirito he applies Roman arches and columns to scan a harmonious interior space. By contrast, Alberti's Tempio Malatestiano with its Roman gravitas, triumphal arch and Vitruvian order is more literally antique, an archaeological revival like that of Mantegna. Perhaps the finest flower of Quattrocento architecture is found in the Ducal Palace of Urbino where a great prince exerted his humanising influence upon art and life, as the Medici did in Florence. Laurana's courtyard there is the acme of the Early Renaissance sense for delicate forms, restrained decoration and equipoise, creating a new beauty by transforming the classical vocabulary. Other landmarks of the Early Renaissance are Alberti's Palazzo Rucellai (Florence), introducing the classical orders in all three storeys. This refined Quattrocento style reaches maturity in the Cancelleria in Rome, whereas in Florence Palazzo Medici and Strozzi were heavily rusticated strongholds. In church architecture the most important event is the centralised and domed structure in place of the longitudinal plan. The Greek-cross church of S. Maria delle Carceri in Prato, by Giuliano da Sangallo, is the first of its kind with an impeccable interior derived from Brunelleschi. Others were to follow: a centralised east end in S. Biagio, Montepulciano, S. Fortunato at Todi and S. Crisostomo at Venice. The Venetian Renaissance was late in conquering the Gothic-Byzantine inheritance. Mauro Coducci and Pietro Lombardo evolved its pristine beauty of abstract geometrical forms in marble clad churches with carved mouldings, dark openings upon white sheets of wall. But for the Byzantine domes, Venetian churches emphasize plane rather than volume and an interrelation of semi-circle and rectangle.

Filippo Brunelleschi was the creator of the Renaissance style in architecture. He is one of the great innovators in quattrocento art, together with Masaccio, Ghiberti and Donatello. Brunelleschi had his roots in the Tuscan Romanesque as well as in the Gothic and in his experience of Roman antiquity. He was first apprenticed to a goldsmith, then tried his hand at sculpture and in emulation of Donatello carved a famous crucifix. After losing the competition for the bronze door of the Florentine Baptistery to Ghiberti he abandoned sculpture for architecture. Gifted

149

136. FLORENCE. *Cathedral cupola*

137. FLORENCE. *Foundling Hospital (Ospedale degli Innocenti)*

with a genius for daring constructional ventures and by a close study of antique methods of vaulting and the handling of stone, he evolved his scheme for the dome of Florence Cathedral, the most coveted commission of the age. It spanned an area of 140 feet across and was built, without wood framework or centering, in horizontal layers of stone and brick.

136
(90, 91)

Its great height resulted in a pointed rather than a spherical shape. Its eight shining ribs, springing from the roots of the octagonal drum, rose in elegant curves up to the ring, their upper terminal, upon which an elaborate marble lantern was built supported by flying buttresses and classical consoles. Brunelleschi's fame was established by this singular feat of engineering by which he constructed the dome as an inner and outer shell, placed lightly upon the great pile of the drum over the crossing, supported by arches and sixteen internal ribs. Its ogival shape, crowned by the shining turret with golden ball and cross dominates the town and the Tuscan hills as memorably as S. Peter's does in Rome.

The elongated and converging ribs of the dome enframing the eight sections are held in place by an ironclad timber hoop at the base, securing its outward thrust. Brunelleschi would have preferred a hemispherical dome like that of the Pantheon. Vasari relates with dramatic momentum the vicissitudes which attended Brunelleschi's building of the dome, the rivalries between him and the influential Ghiberti who as a sculptor was ill qualified to advise on the duomo; marvelling at the technical skills

138. FLORENCE. *Basilica of S. Lorenzo. Interior*

by which Brunelleschi raised the monument to a height of 180 feet from the ground with a passage and stairways between the inner and outer vault, decreasing in weight and thickness, yet capable of supporting the weighty edifice of the lantern. Beneath the drum and echoing the great cupola, he built the semicircular tribunes with shell-topped niches between paired Corinthian columns.

Brunelleschi's inception of a classical style of Renaissance architecture can be seen at its most delicate in the arcaded and vaulted loggia of the Foundling Hospital (Ospedale degli Innocenti) at Florence, built during the early 1420s, manifestation of the new feeling for measure and harmony. These nine arches (with two later additions), supported by slender columns with Corinthian capitals and enframed by end-pilasters, so neatly balanced between the horizontals of steps and continuous entablature beneath the windows and triangular pediments of the first storey, express the very spirit of the Early Renaissance, its nimble grace, its airy serenity. For though rounded arch and colonnade are constituents of Romanesque architecture, their linear rather than sculptural shape, silhouetted against the dark recesses of the vaulted portico, set them apart as a wholly modern creation whose link with antiquity is tenuous. They are closer to Fra Angelico's graceful loggia in the Cortona Annunciation, painted perhaps during the same years and with the same exquisite elegance. Order and

137

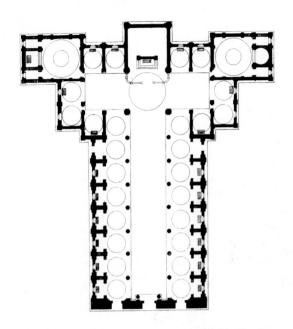

139. FLORENCE.   *S. Lorenzo* (*from Montigny*)

symmetry are the essence of this pristine style and inter-relationship of all forms; as the first floor windows are plumb over the centre of the arches, so the famous roundels of babes in swaddling clothes by Andrea della Robbia in the spandrels echo the semicircular shape of the arches. Brunelleschi's breakthrough to three dimensional forms of Roman columns and generous spacing was still to come. Meanwhile he began to evolve lucid and mathematical ratios of well proportioned longitudinal churches or centrally planned chapels.

Simultaneous with the Cathedral, work went on at S. Lorenzo the Medici church; and here Brunelleschi rebuilt a much older church. He **138** devised a basilica with a broad nave and narrow aisles, separated by arches on Corinthian columns with large protruding impost blocks and a dome over the crossing. The basic module was the square, and the plan **139** is a geometrically precise repetition of this unit. S. Lorenzo is a half-way **(200)** house between Arnolfo's Gothic of S. Croce with its pointed arches and the fully Romanised basilica of S. Spirito of Brunelleschi's last years. The Latin-cross plan of S. Lorenzo is one of calculated precision. The aisles are half the width of the nave and the chapels, flat and rectangular, separated by half-pilasters. The end piers of the nave are composed of lofty fluted pilasters from which are sprung the arches of the crossing. Oculi, arched windows and colonnade relieve the geometrical linearism of S.

140. FLORENCE. *Basilica of S. Croce. Cloisters and Pazzi Chapel*

Lorenzo. As in Early Christian basilicas the nave has a flat coffered ceiling, whereas the lower aisles have domical vaults.

139   The most original part of S. Lorenzo is the Old Sacristy, built between 1421 and 1428 on a central plan, and this in turn is a prelude to the Pazzi Chapel in the courtyard of S. Croce. The spatial division is based on the cube, surmounted by a hemispherical dome with a recessed sancturary, cubic in shape and also domed. Fluted pilasters carry the entrance arch of the altar recess and an ornamental frieze forms part of the entablature beneath the projecting cornice. Roundels, sculpted by Donatello, are set in the centre of the arch spanning the whole width of the wall and also in the pendentives, those 'spherical triangles' supporting the dome. The cubic space of the Sacristy is horizontally divided by structural and decorative elements, basic geometrical shapes like square, semi-circle and triangle, profiled in perfect symmetry upon the white walls of the room.

140   The Pazzi Chapel, in the cloisters of S. Croce, is a more complex building, preceded by a small atrium supporting a panelled storey on Corinthian columns with a high entrance arch in the centre. The gem-like interior develops from the Old Sacristy, but is more masterful, less

154

141. FLORENCE. *S. Spirito.* *Interior (from A. Schutz, Renaissance)*

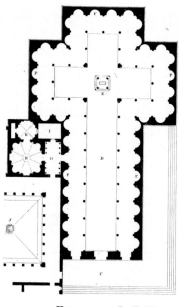

142. FLORENCE. *S. Spirito*
(*from Montigny*)

loaded with decoration. The larger wall spaces are divided by pilasters and continuous cornices in pietra serena, decorated by Luca della Robbia's apostle roundels and symbols. The extended sides of the chapel, including the altar recess correspond with the atrium without, while the central square is crowned by a ribbed dome. The chapel, originally built as a chapter-house in the courtyard of S. Croce is preceded by a temple-like, barrel-vaulted portico. The spacing of triple pilasters within, the ornamental frieze, the colourful roundels of glazed terracotta, rosettes and shell ornament and stained glass windows and the elegant mural partitions contribute to the serene and sober ornateness of the interior.

The Cappella Pazzi was the inspiration to Giuliano da Sangallo's church of S. Maria delle Carceri at Prato, ' the first Renaissance church on a Greek-cross plan with a marble clad exterior and Brunelleschian interior ' (Pevsner).

141
142 But it was in the basilica of S. Spirito that Brunelleschi attained full maturity, transcending the linear and colouristic effect of his earlier designs. Here for the first time sculptural forms prevail in the robustness of nave-columns and arches, the domical aisles and semi-circular chapels. Arcades and clerestorey are of equal height and the ratio of aisle to nave —in height as well as width—is one by two. This instinctive sense of

proportion and the perspective flight of the colonnade towards the altar zone, supported by the great horizontal cornice assures the impression of lucidity and calm. These Corinthian columns and Romanesque arches are raised by high impost blocks and 'fragments of an entablature', syncopated stresses under the flat ceiling with painted coffers. S. Spirito is at the furthest remove from the Gothic; a Renaissance basilica of generous spatial divisions and sculptural forms which are Roman. With its light-flooded cupola over the crossing it is a perfect blend of the cruciform with the centrally planned church.

Brunelleschi was an inexhaustible inventor, an experienced practitioner rather than a theorist like Alberti and Palladio after him. As an architect he dominated the scene in fifteenth century Florence in face of competition and rivalry, Ghiberti's above all, his collaborator at the Duomo whom he eventually supplanted. A friend of Donatello's he had been to Rome with him in his youth (1403) and again in the 1430s to study, survey and measure antique remains. These he explored as a practising architect not as an archaeologist. His sense for geometrical bodies and the classical orders was instinctive, though he worked by strict modules, conceiving architectual space in terms of cubes and hemispheres. There is no trace of literal imitation of classical buildings in his work. It illustrates the true meaning of Renaissance as a 'regrowth', creating a new beauty in art upon the foundations of the past. Brunelleschi was the most influential architect before Bramante and perhaps the greatest that ever lived.

Brunelleschi's influence on palace architecture is chiefly felt in the work of his followers and more especially of Michelozzo, though the Palazzo di Parte Guelfa has been ascribed to him. Here, over a lofty pre-existing base, terminated by an entablature, a second storey was raised around 1435, with two end-pilasters and four arched windows of the grand salone. Corresponding with them are four roundels, destined perhaps for terracottas by della Robbia. All these are characteristic elements of Brunelleschi's style: the delicate mouldings, linear rather than sculptural, the planar recessions of these mouldings, the regular intervals of space between the windows and the noble simplicity of the palace which is without an overhanging roof cornice. Brunelleschi's influence is also felt in the Courtyard of the Medici Palace by Michelozzo, in the wide span of the arches, Tuscan-Romanesque rather than Roman, and the frieze with round armorial bearings, developed from the Ospedale degli Innocenti. There the dominant feature of the façade was its fragility and horizontality based upon the long sequence of arches and the continuous entablature. The architectural members were traced rather than modelled; but in subsequent buildings arches, roundels, pilasters, pediments were given stronger relief and the entablature broken

143. FLORENCE. *Medici-Riccardi Palace*

up and enriched to create the rarefied beauty of cubic and domed spaces like the Cappella Pazzi, one of the summits of the Florentine Quattrocento.

It is a personal language of form, yet without direct reference to Antiquity. That was to come in the Roman colonnades and classic proportions of S. Spirito. Here the trabeation is straight, sweeping boldly towards the altar; the vaulted aisles continue around the transepts and choir, and the Latin-cross basilica is combined with a centralised church. It is the idiom of the future. Only now it becomes possible to speak of Renaissance architecture in the sense in which Alberti understood it, consciously using classical motifs like the Triumphal Arch, and the

144. FLORENCE. *Strozzi Palace*

orders etc. Brunelleschi's proto-Renaissance style, casting off the slough
of the lingering Gothic, grew out of the Romanesque towards a sober
and precise re-creation of classical forms.

Brunelleschi's follower Michelozzi Michelozzo (1396-1472) created
the prototype of the Florentine city palace. A friend of Cosimo Medici
the Elder, he also rebuilt his villas at Careggi and Caffagiolo and reconstructed for him the Dominican Convent of S. Marco, including the
famous library there. Palazzo Medici-Riccardi is a blend of stronghold
and patrician dwelling, an unyielding symmetrical colossus, severe and
imposing, yet graded in texture and topped by an elaborate classical
cornice nearly nine feet wide. Brunelleschian is the shape of the (voussoir)
arches of the ground floor surrounding the tabernacle windows. The
basement is inordinately large compared with the two upper storeys.
No columns or pilasters relieve the solid walls of masonry; string courses
separate the three zones. The principle relief is afforded by the distinction
of materials used, the rusticated irregular blocks below, the channelled
masonry on the *piano nobile* and the smooth cut stone or ashlar on the
top storey. The two upper floors are identical in size and have bifurcated
windows, contained within a semicircular arch, as in the medieval Bargello
or Palazzo della Signoria. These windows are also surrounded by wedge-

143

145. CAREGGI. *Medici Villa*

shaped stones and do not correspond with the large inset arches of the basement.

Party strife and warfare in fifteenth century Florence required such massive palace exteriors, whereas the courtyard within reveals a gentler art of living. Perfectly square and borne aloft by arcades, recalling those of the Innocenti, it is a paragon of Renaissance measure and equipoise. A broad frieze with roundels and garlands forms part of the entablature. These roundels, bearing the Medici arms, are in line with the centre of the arcades and the two-light windows, immediately above the cornice. The corners of the courtyard are not reinforced by piers as in the later courtyard of Urbino, but carried on single columns.

The most formidable Florentine palace in the wake of Michelozzo's example, with variations only in scale and treatment of stone, is that which Filippo Strozzi commissioned from Benedetto da Maiano in 1489. Palazzo Strozzi is truly monolithic, with smooth convex rustication throughout. Its monumental overhang by Cronaca (1536)—grandiloquent symbol of protective power—is superior to Michelozzo's which depresses the upper storey. Cronaca inserted an unadorned frieze beneath the elaborate cornice, calm interval of space, restoring the measured balance of the façade.

144

146. Florence. *Palazzi Pitti. Main façade (photo: E.P.T. Rome)*

Michelozzo created not only the prototype of monumental Florentine palaces, but also the light and elegant Medici villas at Fiesole and Careggi. In 1434 Cosimo il Vecchio requested him to convert a Tuscan stronghold into a plaisance, a country retreat for himself and the meeting place for his cherished Platonists like Marsilio Ficino. To the fortress-like quadrangular building at Careggi with its machicolations **145** and stunted tower, Michelozzo added an arcaded groundfloor wing on the garden side and above it a covered loggia with Ionic columns and straight trabeation, affording wide views over the Tuscan landscape. The main block with small windows and solid walls remained a palatial building, but Michelozzo's graceful Renaissance extension provided an airy summer house for recreation and scholarly gatherings.

The original design of Palazzo Pitti, one of the largest and most **146** imposing of the princely dwellings in Italy has been attributed to Brunel- **(212)** leschi, but also to Alberti. Its nucleus is the central section of the façade comprising seven nobly proportioned window bays. The palace was begun around 1458 by Luca Fancelli and subsequently enlarged. A century later Bartolommeo Ammanati inserted the Renaissance windows within the walled-up arches of the ground floor and added the courtyard on the garden side. Palazzo Pitti is Roman rather than Tuscan, rusticated on all three floors, without divisions by column or pilaster, but varied below by wider spacing and a mezzanine storey. The long rows of superimposed windows and the continuous balusters stress the horizontal of the great

147. Ferrara. *Palazzo dei Diamanti*

palace. Vigorous moulding of enclosing arches and powerful blocks of masonry enhance its robustness, the rhythmical reiteration of openings, its classical symmetry and dignified strength.

In the wake of Florentine palace building, patrician dwellings went up in all the flourishing city states of Italy. Siena can boast the beautiful Palazzo Spannocchi (1470), a small and more compact variation of Palazzo Strozzi and Medici-Riccardi but with an elaborate roof cornice supported by consoles alternating with classical heads. Ten years later Palazzo Bevilacqua was built in Bologna and from it depends the famous Palazzo dei Diamenti in Ferrara begun in the 1490s. This oblong block is entirely clothed in squared and pointed stones, their triangular facets projecting from the wall giving it strength as well as a luminous surface. The monotony of these diamonds is broken by the recessed jambs of the main portal and the carved pilasters flanking it. The latter recur on a grander and more luxuriant scale at the angle of the building, interrupted by the bold corner balcony. A broad frieze divides the two storeys of this monumental palace which is decorated with originality and restraint.

Leon Battista Alberti (1404-72) was the first *uomo universale* of the Renaissance, the type of universally gifted and developed individual which Leonardo brought to fruition. Born in Genoa, the son of a rich and ennobled Florentine merchant, he received the advanced humanist

162

education of the time, having Barzizza for a tutor in whose house he lived with other youths. He was accomplished in every physical and intellectual exercise, running, jumping, ball games and horsemanship; an elegant Latinist, poet, grammarian and mathematician. He studied law in Padua and Bologna, lived mainly in Florence and Rome, but also at the smaller humanist courts of Italy. Like other great men of the Renaissance he had a marked sense of fame and of his own powers, an iron will. His *Ten Books on Architecture* were based on Vitruvius, but without eclecticism. The proportions of the human body provided him with an architectural norm. Like Leonardo he revered the beauty of man and of nature and in his own person combined grace with strength. He associated with the best of his time, humanists, artists, popes and princes; Lionello d'Este Federico da Montefeltro and the Gonzaga of Mantua were among his patrons. He dedicated his book on painting to Brunelleschi.

In Florence he moved in the circle of Ghiberti, Donatello, Masaccio. In Rome Nicholas V employed him at the Curia. Architecture was only one of his many interests. His pioneering influence in this field was confined to one palace and four churches, and these he designed while others built them. His architectural *début* was Palazzo Rucellai, Florence **148** (1446-51) which Bernardo Rossellino executed, the second of the great Renaissance palaces after Michelozzo's Palazzo Medici. They share certain characteristics like the round headed windows and the over-hanging roof cornice; but there are great differences between them. Alberti's palace design is essentially planar and linearistic. The flat surfaces of smooth stone are built up in perspective foreshortening and divided by three orders of superimposed pilasters with a sequence of Doric, Ionian and Corinthian capitals. The pilasters are wall divisions as well as ornaments, like the two crests, so elegantly placed in line with the two entrances. The balance of verticals and horizontals is based on classical entablatures separating the storeys. An architrave resting on a small column divides the windows into a rounded top with two arches above a rectangle. The ground floor has a reticulated base with low projecting benches and two heavily encased doorways.

Palazzo Rucellai presents a frontage where all the elements flow into a delicate network of lines and the overall effect is pictorial rather than structural on account of the smooth rustication, the noble propor-tions, the calculated symmetry of all parts where the pilasters determine the size of the storeys. It is a classical building, refined, becalmed, withdrawn into its own harmonies and composed of alternating rhythms of channelled masonry, friezes and cornices, a kind of visual music.

But the work by which Alberti is chiefly remembered is the Tempio **149** Malatestiano at Rimini, built to commemorate the local tyrant Sigismondo

148. FLORENCE. *Palazzo Rucellai (photo: Russo/E.P.T. Florence)*

149. RIMINI. *Tempio Malatestiano*

Malatesta and Isotta degli Atti, his mistress and later his wife. In 1450
Sigismondo decided to rebuild the Gothic church of S. Francesco and
Alberti drew up plans transforming it into a Roman temple. As it was
impossible to change the Gothic interior, except by the addition of six
chapels, a task which fell to Matteo de' Pasti and Agostino di Duccio **150**
the sculptor, Alberti undertook to encase the Gothic edifice in a Roman
shell. The triumphal arch motif seemed to him most fitting for the
glorification of the ruler and this he employed three times on the façade.
The flanking arches were to shelter the tombs of Isotta and Sigismondo,
but special chapels were built for them inside the church. Alberti designed
a deep central archway and in the shadow within it the entrance door,
with a Roman pediment and geometrical patterns of disks and squares
in the spaces above. The triumphal arch corresponds to the lofty nave,
while the side arches indicate the lower aisles. Alberti planned a great
hemispherical dome like that of the Roman Pantheon, as we know from
a medal by Matteo de' Pasti. The façade was to contain another arch
above the entrance of which only the pilasters remain. The other main
features are the four half-columns, continued by pilasters in the second
storey, and rising from a high base which isolates the temple from the
world around it. Projecting cornice and entablature break the continuity
of the columns, just as the entrance archway interrupts their common

165

150 RIMINI. *Tempio Malatestiano. Interior*

base. These fluted half-columns with their rich capitals of curling
foliage, scrolls and heads of antique genii and the judiciously placed
garlands are the chief ornament of the façade.

As the blind arches are supported by pilasters, so the grand arcades
on the sides of the temple are carried by square piers, according to Alberti's
theory of their function. He looked upon columns as ornaments rather
than weight-bearing supports, to be incorporated into the wall, not left
free-standing as in Brunelleschi's loggia. The entablature between arch
and pier is continued all around the building as is the ornamental frieze
at the base. Sarcophagi of illustrious men, poets and humanists were
placed into the external niches. Even the corner pier is not stressed or
strengthened, except by greater width and an inscription plate. Garlanded
disks in the spandrels are the only ornament in this austere temple,

151. FLORENCE. *S. Maria Novella. Facade*

inspired by Roman monuments like the Arch of Constantine and the Colosseum. Other than Palazzo Rucellai the Malatestiano is a powerful, three-dimensional structure, richer in volumes, greater in contrasts of light and shade. It has a heavy gait and a learned archaeological flavour, in marked contrast to the bright and spacious interior of the Franciscan church, with its enchanting relief sculpture by Agostino di Duccio and his school.

Alberti's next work was again commissioned by Giovanni Rucellai and is also a modernisation of an older church. The façade of S. Maria Novella (after 1456) is a reincarnation of S. Miniato al Monte, that landmark of the Tuscan Romanesque on the hill above the River Arno. The same multicoloured marble is used for geometrical pattern. Here, as there, a classical gable crowns the centre portion, marking the nave, whilst scrolls indicate the aisles. The whole area of the façade is circumscribed by a square, subdivided in the lower half by further squares on either side of the Roman doorway, flanked by half-columns on pedestals. This exquisite marble-clad temple frontage has a lace-like wheel pattern inside the scrolls and is framed by zebra-coloured piers at the sides.

* * * * *

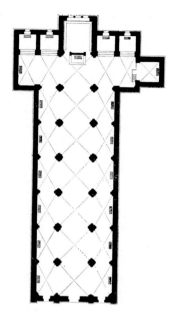

152.   Florence.   S. Maria
Novella (from Montigny)

During the last decades of his life, Alberti designed two more churches in Mantua, both for the Gonzaga: S. Sebastiano (1460) and S. Andrea (1470).   In S. Maria Novella he had adjusted his style to Florentine environment, and at Rimini to Roman precedent in the Arch of Augustus. Here at Mantua he was free to pursue his own ideas unhampered by pre-existing structures.   In S. Sebastiano he adopted a Greek, in S. Andrea a Latin-cross plan.   Both façades are based on the square and both have pilasters and pediments, but no longer half-columns.   In S. Sebastiano there is a large expanse of blank wall with small openings into the bays; S. Andrea has an enormous triumphal arch entrance, echoed above the pediment by another arch and accompanied by windows and niches on either side; also a giant and a smaller order of pilasters.   The colossal arch motif is carried over into the aisleless interior with its tunnel-like nave, domed crossing and barrel-vaulted chapels, three on either side of the nave.   This type of vaulting stems from the Roman Baths and the Basilica of Maxentius.   This vast coffered vault is not carried by columns or arches, but by the walls of the nave, transformed into piers through the insertion of large chapels.

Archaeology, mathematics and a re-interpretation of Vitruvian theory of architecture conditioned Alberti's approach to Antiquity in contrast to Brunelleschi's practical interest in the nature of classical building

153. MANTUA. *S. Sebastiano*

methods. The Malatestiano was a reconstruction of a Roman temple
without colonnades, and the marble façade of S. Maria Novella a classical
mask concealing a Gothic church. The Tempio remained an isolated
phenomenon without succession, but façades in polychrome marble,
based on simple mathematical ratios, became the vogue in Renaissance
Florence; while in Mantua the domed one-aisled interior of S. Andrea
with chapels at the sides, anticipated the vast Jesuit churches of the future.

Alberti's pupil and acting hand, especially in the construction of
Palazzo Rucellai was Bernardo Rossellino (1409-64), sculptor and architect
whom the humanist Pope Pius II employed to transform his native village

154. MANTUA. *Basilica of S. Andrea*

155. MANTUA. *Basilica of S. Andrea.* *Interior*

of Corsignano into the township of Pienza by building a cathedral and palaces around a city square. This was an urbanistic project unique in its single-mindedness and stylistic harmony. Rossellino's masterpiece was the new Cathedral with flanking palaces converging towards the **156** town hall opposite. Nave and aisles were of equal height and the façade

158. Pienza. *Palazzo Pubblico*

159. PERUGIA. *S. Bernardino (photo: Gabinetto Fotografico Nazionale, Rome)*

S. Bernardino at Perugia by Agostino di Duccio. This is not surprising, **159**
for Agostino was the principal sculptor of the relief decorations inside
the Tempio and intimately acquainted with its structure. The Oratory
retains the triumphal arch motive which spans enough space for a double
door, giving scope in its large tympanum, arch, friezes and flanking
pilasters to a profusion of delicate relief sculpture. The remaining wall
spaces are filled with shallow tabernacles containing figures in both
storeys. The gabled oratory façade is a linear and ornamental translation
of faintly Albertian forms, but it is the delicacy of low reliefs rather than
structural aspirations which give it distinctive character.

160-161. NAPLES. *Castel Nuovo with Triumphal Arch*

162. URBINO. *Ducal Palace. West front*

Albertian forms are also reflected in a monument of a very different nature built during the same decade (1453-66) in the city of Naples: the Triumphal Arch of Alfonso of Aragon. This was probably designed **160** by Pietro da Milano and richly decorated by a host of sculptors from all over Italy. Architecturally the monument consists of a closely knit sequence of storeys with Roman arches between raised and fluted twin-columns on Albertian lines and a central frieze celebrating the triumphal **161** entry of King Alfonso into Naples. This ornamental entrance to the Castel Nuovo is inserted between two sturdy machicolated keeps and it resembles the 'torricini' enframing the loggias at the Urbino palace façade. Every available wall surface is overlaid with figure sculpture or ornament of many styles from the griffins and Victories in the spandrels to the Virtues in shell-niches and the river gods of the scroll-like tympanum. This encrustation deflects from the architectural merits of the monument and its balanced divisions. Columns and pilasters have no supporting function, being used, as Alberti commended, as the chief ornaments of a building. Alfonso's arch

177

163. URBINO. *East front and entrance forecourt*

with its many classical elements presents a link between the architectural styles then developing at Rimini and Urbino.

But the grandest and most accomplished of all Renaissance palaces is Federico da Montefeltro's Palazzo Ducale at Urbino. Nor was it simply a palace alongside a street, but a complex of buildings of different periods on a disparate hilly site overlooking the valley, true symbol of the Renaissance city state—*una città in forma di palazzo*—as Castiglione wrote in his *Cortegiano*. Its story is intricate and protracted. It has been told with rare ingenuity by Pasquale Rotondi who distinguishes three major phases: a medieval foundation which successive architects of Duke Federico transformed into the present fastness of castle cum palace, reflecting more than any other building in Italy the humanist spirit and the social graces of an Early Renaissance court. This was due to the master plan of Luciano Laurana, an architect from Dalmatia and to the changes and interior decorations of Francesco di Giorgio from Siena and a host of Tuscan and Lombard sculptors working under his direction, but perhaps

164. URBINO. *Ducal Palace. Grand Courtyard*

most of all to the unique personality of the Duke of Urbino. His palace
became a princely dwelling with a host of stately rooms, grand staircase,
inner courtyard, gardens, a chapel, library and study, reflecting the
love of the liberal arts by an enlightened Renaissance ruler.

As the leader of his small city-state and later as Gonfaloniere of the
Church, Federico held the balance of power in central Italy and, by his
wide humanist and artistic interests, created a cultural centre comparable
to that of Medicean Florence. Piero della Francesca painted his portrait
and the same artist left his imprint on the style of the palace building;
proof of that is seen in the architectural setting of his *Flagellation*, still at
Urbino, or of the Brera Madonna with Duke Federico. Piero as well
as Alberti were favoured guests at the court of Urbino during the inception
of the new building.

The palace stands on a high eminence and its principal features
are the twin towers or torricini on the west front, framing and buttressing
a narrow façade. These cylindrical towers have a pointed top and octagonal base supported by brackets. The centre of the façade consists of
superimposed loggias, coffered vaulting and is crowned by a canopy. The
castle-like west façade with its two keeps and an adjoining square tower
form an enclosed terrace at the level of the second storey, the Terrazza del
Gallo, with finely proportioned arches on slender columns. Exterior arches
and ornamental windows match those within the palace. The long east **163**

165. URBINO. *Ducal Palace. Sala degli Angeli*

front which is the earliest has still Gothic bifurcate or mullion windows of smaller size, whereas in the entrance forecourt the three portals and four large windows are not only rhythmically spaced in relation to each other but also connected by carved friezes, inscribed stone slabs under the sills and upon the lintels and framed by fluted or ornamental pilasters. The ground floor of this wing is built of rusticated stone in colourful contrast to the brickwall texture of the upper storey. A letter patent was issued by Duke Federico in 1468 appointing Luciano Laurana to be architect in charge, but the latter may have worked there some years prior to that date. By 1472 Laurana had left Urbino and Francesco di Giorgio took over.

Apart from the façade, the exquisite suite of living rooms and the famous Studiolo of Federico, the consummate masterpiece in the palace is the Grand Courtyard, the noblest in Italy. It is a square space ' with a light springy arcade of Corinthian columns echoed by shallow pilasters between the windows on the upper storey ' (Pevsner). A frieze in Roman lettering dedicated to the Duke runs beneath both cornices which form a continuous base for the windows. Round disks mark the pendentives between the arches, supporting a lofty cross vault. A much vaunted feature of the Cortile are the angle piers of twin pilasters with only a narrow space between them and with adjoining columns on either side. This ingenious device provides a strong wall-support at the turning of the corners in the courtyard, as organic as it is graceful. For Florentine palaces had only a single column to support the arches at the corners.

164

The courtyard at Urbino combines resilience with grace, strength with harmony, and equilibrium of mind and matter which the humanity of Federico and the skill of his artists imprinted upon the palace architecture. Notwithstanding the vastness of the building and the incongruities of its growth, it has proportions related to man and a wealth of exquisite ornaments wrought by many hands. Florence apart, it is at Urbino that the delicate and shapely art of the quattrocento appears at its purest.

In the interior decoration of the resplendent rooms, halls, landings, **165** ceilings, door frames and chimneypieces the architectural style of Piero's paintings is reflected, and more especially in the crisp design of capitals on pilasters and columns, the disks and marble panellings of walls. One need only compare the writhing acanthus leaves and scrolls of a Corinthian capital in the Grand Courtyard of the palace with that in the Arezzo *Annunciation* or the cornices, door frames and the slabs of inlaid marble with those of Urbino, to become aware of Piero's influence.

The chief glory of the interior architecture in the palace are the delicately carved and infinitely varied arabesques of vine leaves, cupids, urns, garlands and ducal emblems, the impeccable vaulted ceilings and console brackets and the intarsia relating the military and humanistic life of Federico. But closest to Piero's cool geometrical classicism is the Cappella del Perdono, a translation into real architectural space and form of the painted apse and coffered vault, the slabs of coloured marble alternating with pilasters which enshrine the Madonna and Saints in the Brera altarpiece. The disk motif and briskly sprung arches and projecting cornices and entablatures of the Urbino palace have their protagonists in Piero's Arezzo frescoes and in the Flagellation picture. Perhaps it is forcing a point if the asymmetrical arrangement of figures and architecture of the latter in an overall harmony of space has been likened to the irregular lay-out of the Urbino palace, resolved in the twin towers of the west facade, providing a central pivot in a building which otherwise straddles an irregular complex of wings and inner courts to the north and south. Yet Laurana's and Francesco di Giorgio's unified palace of Urbino is the architectural and decorative equivalent of Piero's paintings, both, in their several media, the quintessence of the quattrocento style.

Laurana was conversant with the works of Brunelleschi and Alberti and he moved Renaissance architecture on to a new plane; externally by the sovereign use of Alberti's triumphal arch and internally by the rarefied design of architectural members, the splendour of well proportioned halls with ornamented soffits or vaulted ceilings, their pendentives resting on carved consoles or of the smaller rooms destined for meditation and study, hung with the portraits of illustrious men, expressing the

166. PESARO. *Palazzo della Prefettura*

humanist passion of the age.

In the Grand Courtyard, departing from Brunelleschi's loggias in the Innocenti, Laurana used contrasts of light and colour, opposing the shaded arcades to the bright wall surfaces and the radiant pilasters and friezes to the mellow red of the brick walling. The exhilaration which the courtyard inspires derives from the felicitous proportions, the rhythm of spatial intervals, the Neo-Attic shapes in the luminous and airy enclosures, the concord and proportions of all the parts of the building, so that nothing could be added or taken away without destroying the unity of the whole (Alberti). The courtyard at Urbino attained this degree of integration by a wholly original concept of classical art. It is from these premises that Bramante and Raphael, both born at Urbino—and the former certainly present during the years of palace construction—evolved the later stages of Renaissance architecture.

166 The Palazzo della Prefettura at Pesaro, completed in 1475 for Alessandro Sforza, comes within the context of the palace of Urbino; especially in the exquisite window surrounds with their fluted pilasters, trabeation, frieze and garland bearing cupids. The open arcade, groin vaulted, and supported by block-like piers is like the sub-structure of a Romanesque town hall. But the archivolts are recessed and finely carved as are the garlands in the spandrels. These decorative carvings recall

167. SAN LEO (*Pesaro*). *The Rocca*

Francesco di Giorgio's work in nearby Urbino. The main feature of Palazzo Pesaro is its wilful lack of symmetry; for the five elaborate windows are not placed in line with the round arches or wreathed disks. Yet the large blank wall spaces between the cornices restore the balance of the façade and its pleasing proportions, based on horizontal divisions which add up to a harmonious synthesis of identical units. Moreover the weightiness of the rectangular frontage, screening a large hall in the *piano nobile*, is lightened by the delicate mouldings and Renaissance windows.

Francesco di Giorgio's sense of exquisite design, so evident in the interior decorations of the Urbino palace, and more especially in the elegant consoles, the diaphanous ceilings and stuccoed chimneys is reflected again in the domed interior of S. Maria del Calcinaio, Brunelleschian in its lucid silhouetting of arches, pilasters, cornices in grey pietra serena upon the radiant walls. Francesco was equally gifted as sculptor, painter, architect and military engineer and wrote a famous *Trattato di Architettura civile e militare*. To him are ascribed the Ducal palace at Gubbio, the town hall at Jesi and several churches at Siena and Urbino. Not the least original among his works are the bastions he built for Federico da Montefeltro who was locked in life-long combat with Sigismondo Malatesta, tyrant of Rimini, whom he eventually defeated. The two strongholds in the Marches, the Rocca di San Leo and Sassocorvaro combine an

168. SASSOCORVARO (*Pesaro*). *The Fortress*

impregnable structure with organic landscape siting and a powerful
aesthetic functionalism.

Memories of the Torricini in the Palace of Urbino may have inspired
167 the towers of San Leo, smooth like the bare rocks and poised ' like a
gigantic bird spreading its wings ' upon a steep and precipitous cliff
of immense height. A chain of machicolations runs along the upper
register of walls and towers, and the fortress, crowning the summit of a

169. ROME. *Palazzo Venezia* (*photo: Italian Institute, London*)

rocky escarpment, is built on different levels like the substructure of S. Francesco at Assisi. Precariously placed on a narrow site facing the gorge, it seems to grow out of the rugged rockface, tied by a nimble belt of cornices.

Sassocorvaro has even greater formal unity, a powerful massive **168** mould of circular shape, not unlike the elliptic drum of a church which Francesco built at Urbino, the Oratory of S. Bernardino, but transposed onto a huge scale. This compact mass of rounded shapes is articulated only by four gyrating cornices, and the space between them is graded in circumference towards the bulging top. Its spherical bulk stands firmly on a broad base, leaving a concave middle section, perfectly plain except for small windows under the roof. No enemy could gain a foothold on the smooth outer walls, either in the high basement or the wasp-waist centre or overhanging crown. Basically this formidable stronghold is of cylindrical shape whose Roman brick walling comes alive with a rotating movement which precludes all rigidity. In the history of military architecture Francesco di Giorgio holds a unique place, harmonising rock and ' rocca ' in complete visual unity and giving his fortresses strength as well as shapeliness.

Florence is the city of Quattrocento palaces whilst Rome was shaped by the architects of the High Renaissance and the Baroque. There are

170. ROME. *Palazzo della Cancelleria (photo: E.N.I.T. Rome)*

169   only two major palaces of the fifteenth century in Rome and both depend from Leon Battista Alberti, Palazzo Venezia and the Cancelleria or papal chancellery. The former is a huge, fortress-like rectangular pile of a building with battlements and a square tower, quite plain, except for the central balcony and entrance door. But the courtyard has a two-storey arcade and the round arches are carried by columns on high bases attached to the piers, a motif from the Colosseum which Alberti also used on the façade of the Malatestiano. Alberti did not build this palace, but he may have designed it.

170   The same applies to the Cancelleria which is more closely related to Palazzo Rucellai in Florence, his only authentic palace. It was built by an unknown architect around 1489 for Cardinal Riario and repeats Alberti's double pilasters enframing the window bays in alternating spatial rhythms. But the pilasters do not rise from the base of the building where the masonry is more weighty and the windows are smaller and unadorned. Bold cornices stress the horizontal of the long frontage. The articulation by flat pilasters with Corinthian capitals and the overall smoothness of surfacing link the Cancelleria to Palazzo Rucellai, though the window surrounds are more elegant, the profiles more subtle and tenuous. Also the sparing ornaments and their positioning betray the hand of a master: the elaborate classical gateway and balcony, balanced by a second entrance with a heavy lintel on consoles, or the cunningly

186

171. VENICE. *Cà d'Oro*

placed rosettes above the arched windows all along the *piano nobile*. The inner courtyard reveals an architect familiar with Laurana's cortile in the Palace of Urbino; but here, two arcades of the same proportions are superimposed, supporting an upper storey on classical columns, and

172. VENICE. *Palazzo Corner Spinelli (from O. Raschdorff, Venedig)*

repeating the pilaster motif and disk rosettes of the façade. As at Urbino the corners are strengthened by piers, not carried by single columns. Grace and elegance of the Cancelleria are a legacy of Florence as well as Urbino, prelude and transition to the more massive High Renaissance palaces of Rome.

Venetian palaces, far into the fifteenth century (Ca' d'Oro, Palazzo Foscari, Palazzo Fasan) were still of the florid Gothic type with their tracery windows, pinnacles, balconies. As there was no space for an inner courtyard as in Florence or Rome, all the splendour was lavished on the façades and the lofty state-room windows in the central section of

173. VENICE. *Palazzo Vendramin Calergi (from O. Raschdorff, Venedig)*

174. VENICE. *S. Michele in Isola (photo: Alinari/E.P.T. Venice)*

175. VENICE. *S. Maria dei Miracoli* (*photo: Italian Institute, London*)

the building and the large openings at the water's edge. Ca' d'Oro was
built on the Canale Grande between 1427 and 1436, and here the hollowing
out of masonry, the delicate carving of quatrefoil crosses, disks and ogee
arches is carried over into all three storeys, leaving only a narrow section
of solid walling on one side of the palace. Wall surfaces are dissolved by
subtle lacework in stone, flamboyant arches and merlons and by the
vertical linearism of balusters and colonettes. The exquisite detail of
carved frieze and cornices, the stone tracery on doors and windows, flame-
like and curvilinear shapes, contained within a framework of square
and rectangle, redress the essential imbalance of the most beautiful façade
in Venice. Like all Venetian palaces it is composed of arched portals at
the level of the water and open loggias and balconies in the two upper
storeys, screening the central living room across the whole width of the
palace from which the pageant life on the Canale could be watched.

In the latter half of the fifteenth century two architects reached
prominence in Venice: Mauro Coducci and Pietro Lombardo. Their
palaces (Corner Spinelli and Vendramin Calergi) divide the façade more
evenly in size and spacing, abandoning ogee windows for large round bays
separated by columns. Palazzo Vendramin is the most classical and
imposing before the coming of Jacopo Sansovino. The square block with
its five identical bays in the two upper storeys, with balconies and large
mullion windows, the sculptural vigour of engaged columns, paired at the
side to stress the importance of the centre, compose a building based on
ordered symmetry and decorative restraint. Yet the interweaving of
circle and rectangle, of sunlit projections and shaded recessions, the
reduction of solid wall spaces and the fleeting reflections in the lagoon,
enhance the effects of spatial mystery.

Contrasts of white marble and black water, of coloured inlay and
weathered stone play their part in Quattrocento architecture at Venice;
flat pattern rather than structural form. The façade of S. Michele in
Isola, designed by Coducci with exceptional sensibility, speaks a pictorial
language where dark apertures pierce the white rusticated walls rising
near the water's edge. It is a shallower version of Alberti's Tempio
façade with a high rectangle screening the nave between squared pilasters
and crowned by a large lunette, a geometrical design of pristine beauty
and purity.

S. Michele is a tentative beginning; its concept comes to maturity
and fruition in the uncommonly lofty façade of S. Zaccaria. Coducci
repeats the crowning lunette and curvilinear buttresses, but now in more
elaborate fashion with several orders of twin columns and double pilasters
between arched openings or blind niches. Richly carved friezes and
cornices break up the planar wall surfaces and the façade builds up,

176. VENICE. *S. Zaccaria* (*from F. Ongania. Streets and Canals in Venice*)

tapering and organic, from a broad podium in six registers towards the
great oculus window under the deeply moulded lunette arch.

But the finest example of the Veneto Byzantine fusion with the
175 Renaissance is S. Maria dei Miracoli. Built by Pietro Lombardo between
1481 and 1489, it has an elaborate exterior of coloured marble panelling
with inlaid disks, squares, crosses and blind arcades. Dark mouldings
of pilasters, resilient arches and projecting cornices symmetrically divide
the planes, and the rectangular body of the church has two storeys and
an all-embracing lunette over the façade, a small dome over the sanctuary.

177. VENICE. *School of S. Mark's (from A. Schutz, Renaissance)*

In the axial centre of the lunette around the large oculus small disk windows gyrate. As the space is restricted, the divisions and architectural members are painterly rather than sculptural to simulate an impression of sheerness and size.

To sum up: Venetian Quattrocento architecture, like no other in Italy, was conditioned by the long survival of Byzantine and Gothic styles and by the ever present model of the Doge's Palace and its double arcades with trefoil apertures and solid walling above. In Venice walls rise high and sheer from street pavement or water surface. Colour-contrasts depend on the white Istrian stone and window openings reflecting the dark lagoon. Walls are organised by deep mouldings rather than architectural members; the emphasis is on colour rather than line. Circular forms and panelled rectangles combine. Gothic loggias and windows are transformed now into long and narrow openings (S. Zaccaria) or **176** into wide mullion windows (Palazzo Corner and Vendramin) formed by **172, 173**

178. BERGAMO. *Colleoni Chapel (from A. Schutz, Renaissance)*

179. PAVIA. *Certosa*

an architrave cutting across two semi-circular halves with a disk window
on top of the central pillar.   At the Scuola di S. Marco Lombardo's
screen-like façade combines many elements of the Quattrocento in Venice:
the fusion of oblongs and semicircles, lunettes over doors and protruding
roof cornice, triangular tympanum windows, squared marble sheeting
and *trompe-l'oeil* niches.   Architectural forms are used decoratively
rather than functionally until the Renaissance restores weight and the
classical orders.

   The Lombard Renaissance which culminated in an architect of
genius, Donato Bramante whose work matured in Rome though it began
in Milan, evolved from the International Gothic; and Giovanni Antonio
Amadeo (1447-1522).   Almost exactly coeval with Bramante, Amadeo's
style is more typically Lombard by dint of its decorative qualities.   His
best works are the Colleoni Chapel at Bergamo and, in collaboration with
Mantegazza, his contribution to the Certosa of Pavia.   From 1466 he
worked at the terracotta ornaments in the two cloisters of the Certosa and
after 1473 he was co-architect of the Certosa façade and in sole charge of
it from 1491.   Amadeo was a sculptor-architect and wholly dedicated
to combining and unifying the two media, in harmony with Lombard
taste for profuse decoration.   His wall surfaces are so encrusted with
sculptural relief and polychrome marble that the plastic and three-
dimensional qualities of architecture are almost obliterated, in contrast
to the Florentine genius for clear definition.

The Colleoni Chapel which the Venetian general commissioned in 1470 as his mausoleum, adjoining the Cathedral and claiming the old sacristy for its site, is a conspicuous edifice in red, black and white marble with an octagonal drum, cupola, pinnacled turrets and a row of niche-sculptures above an open gallery of late Gothic design. But the main body of the chapel, in spite of recessed windows and small doorway, lunettes and two lateral niches with busts of emperors, is a cubic block with surface planes entirely overlaid with ornaments; framed by corner pilasters with disks and diamond shapes. Every inch of the wall is covered either by geometrical patterns, or blossoms out in reliefs or statuettes between oblong panels with urns of fruit and writhing foliage. The windows are filled with small columns and flanked by pilasters.

At Bergamo such *embarras de richesses* is wholly integrated, whereas
the Certosa of Pavia is a product of many styles. This Carthusian monastery was founded by the Visconti dynasty in 1396 as their memorial, and mainly completed by 1492. But work at the façade continued into the sixteenth century. Amadeo's share was the richly ornamented lower half of the façade up to the first cornice, though the severely classical doorway is by Briosco. The two blind and two open windows and their sculptural surrounds with niche figures and friezes and the corner buttresses are the most resplendent part of the façade which rises from a base with marble roundels, carved with Roman emperors, and oblong relief panels above. In contrast to the quiet upper section, the total decoration of Amadeo presents the most elaborate fusion of sculpture with architecture before the Baroque. But the main stream of Renaissance architecture did not flow in the *città alta* of Bergamo, nor in the plain of Pavia, but in Florence and in Rome, where Bramante and Raphael, in rivalry with Michelangelo, were to realize their heroic concept of classic art.

In his fundamental essay *Architectural Principles in the Age of Humanism*, Professor Rudolf Wittkower has explored the metaphysical and mathematical background of the centrally planned church, based upon the human figure, standing with arms extended and contained within circle and square. We know this Vitruvian figure from many Renaissance drawings by Francesco di Giorgio, Leonardo and others. Its relationship to architecture which was to be organic like the human body is one of the chief tenets of antiquity and also of the Renaissance. Man, the measure of all things, could be circumscribed in his natural proportions by the ideal geometrical form of the circle, surrounded by a square and this formula was applied to the ground plan of the ideal church. The Vitruvian postulate that the proportions of the human figure should be mirrored in the proportions of the temple was applied to Christian churches by the architects of humanism. The circular building had

180. PRATO (Firenze). *S. Maria delle Carceri*

religious significance; man within the circle, 'the mathematical sympathy between microcosm and macrocosm', between man and world, man and his god was established. In practice roundness could be modified by polygonal forms, or rectangular chapels added to the circle, producing the Greek-cross plan. Early Christian churches like S. Stefano Rotondo and S. Costanza, the Lateran and Florentine Baptisteries were either round or octagonal. In the Renaissance longitudinal churches were disapproved of, though a blending of domed crossing and longitudinal nave was not excluded.

o

181. POGGIO A CAIANO. *Villa Medici*

Though Leonardo built no churches of his own, his sketchbooks
illustrate his preoccupation with domes surrounded by a wealth of
hemispherical chapels, clustering like minarets around a central core,
an infinite variety of shapes, rounded or polygonal or with a centralised
east end only. The first Renaissance church on a Greek-cross plan with
a dome and short rectangular arms is Giuliano da Sangallo's S. Maria
delle Carceri at Prato (1485). Giuliano was the most gifted of Brunel-
180 leschi's folowers and S. Maria delle Carceri is a variation on the theme
of the Pazzi Chapel. Its plan is a circle enclosed by a square, above
which a ribbed dome hovers lightly on pendentive supports. The square
is extended on all four sides by the short arms of the chapels. The interior
differs from the Cappella Pazzi by the stressed corner pilasters in dark
pietra serena, supporting the arches at the joints. Here, as there, a
continuous frieze and entablature move around the white walls of the
church. Externally S. Maria delle Carceri is a synthesis of regular bodies
—a cylindrical drum seated on a cube under a shallow dome—a compact
and unified shell, enclosing volume. The radiant walls are patterned by

CHAPTER FIVE

HIGH RENAISSANCE ARCHITECTURE AND
MANNERISM 1500—1600

The High Renaissance takes root in Rome with the coming of Bramante in 1500. Round and domed churches, coffered vaults and massive palaces characterize the new style. Bramante's Tempietto, though small in size, is conceived in terms of volume and sculptural form, a cylindrical body, hemispherical dome and circular colonnade. The monumental reconstruction of S. Peter's occupies the best talent of the century. Bramante's Greek-cross plan and dome had to await the modified realisation of Michelangelo. His grandiose Belvedere Court with massed arcades, exedra and a theatre was only begun. The greatest palace in Rome, Palazzo Farnese by his follower Antonio da Sangallo, completed by Michelangelo, showed the beginning of Mannerist features. Raphael's favourite pupil, Giulio Romano, once he had exchanged Rome for Mantua, evolved a titanic dynamism in his stunted palaces, bending classical elements to his own will and fancy. But the mainspring of Mannerist architecture is Michelangelo's Medici Chapel and Laurentian Library in Florence. Here even the columns are embedded in walls, without supporting function, windows are blind, consoles and pilasters mere ornaments. Michelangelo's genius transcends and defeats classification. He remains the chief representative of the High Renaissance as well as the begetter of Mannerism and of the Baroque. But the graceful elegancies of Peruzzi's Palazzo Massimi or of Villa Giulia—combined effort of Vignola, Vasari and Ammanati—constitute a new and exhilarating style where classical motifs are freely, almost playfully handled. In the north Sansovino, Sanmicheli and Palladio all belong to the High Renaissance. In Palladio classic art is reborn; his powerful palaces and church facades derive from Imperial Roman art. In his villas of the Veneto geometrical planning, cubic forms and temple porticoes blend with the landscape, generating a mood of their own.

It is of great significance that the first architect of the High Renaissance Donato Bramante (1444-1514) grew up at Urbino, the city of Piero della Francesca, Laurana and Francesco di Giorgio, at a time when the great Montefeltro palace was being rebuilt. Bramante associated with the most advanced painters and architects of the day at the court of Duke Federico, the most enlightened and erudite patron of the arts, and began his career as a painter under the likely tutelage of Piero della Francesca, Mantegna and Francesco di Giorgio. By 1481 he was in the employ of Lodovico Sforza in Milan where he spent nearly twenty years in close communion with Leonardo. Thus Bramante was favoured by birth and circumstance to promote the transformation of the Early into the High Renaissance.

His first Milanese buildings were under the spell of Leonardo's obsessive designs of circular and polygonal structures, but he also re-membered Alberti's domed longitudinal churches and Mantegna's bold

185. MILAN. *S. Maria presso S. Satiro (photo: Costa/E.P.T. Milan)*

experiments in perspective illusion. These were the elements he used in
185 S. Maria presso S. Satiro in Milan, with its broad Roman arches and
ornate pilasters supporting the coffered vault of the cupola. The feigned
apse behind the altar is only a painted relief, a piece of architectural
illusionism to enlarge the restricted space of the sanctuary. The adjoining
Baptistery is centrally planned and has an elegant matroneum or women's
gallery over arcaded shell niches, separated by a frieze of cupids and busts

186. MILANO. *S. Maria delle Grazie. Cloisters and cupola*

187. ROME. *S. Maria della Pace. Cloisters (photo: Gabinetto Fotografico Nazionale, Rome)*

of Roman emperors. Pilasters and entablatures have florid patterns in the ornamental style of the Lombards. The plan of the Baptistery is of great consequence for the future, because it is a Greek cross inscribed in a circle.

186 But Bramante's greatest work at Milan was the building of a central-ised east end in Solari's late Gothic Latin-cross church S. Maria delle Grazie. He was active at this task during the years when Leonardo was painting his *Last Supper* in the refectory. The exterior of the rounded apse and sixteen sided cupola, grafted upon a large cubic base, profusely decorated by wheel windows, twin arches and medallions, is an imposing structure with projecting apses on three sides. This complex of cube and cylinders encloses a spacious interior, a square crossing and luminous altar zone with decorative arcades and pendentives supporting the dome, an ordered complex of massive masonry, articulated by majestic arches and vaults. The centrally planned east end is attached to a long low nave.

Externally S. Maria delle Grazie is distinguished by the great square over the crossing, covered by a high drum, polygonal dome and lantern with circular apses in place of transepts. The roofing of the dome is shallow. Yet the effect of the whole with its Tuscan arcades and Lombard wall decorations which leave no surface plain, is monumental. While at Milan Bramante also built the cloisters adjoining S. Ambrogio, the Canons' Cloister and another with Doric columns on high plinths and wide arches springing from dosserets, contrasted by a small upper storey with windows unrelated to the arches. Here the clear definition of architectural members presages Bramante's Roman style.

With the fall of Lodovico Sforza at the hand of the French in 1499, both Leonardo and Bramante withdrew from Milan. A great future lay before the architect in Rome with the reign of Pope Julius II (1503-13) who initiated the rebuilding of S. Peter's and of the Vatican. But even before that Bramante was engaged on two commissions which show the immediate impact of Rome upon his first Lombard manner. The novelty in the small cloister of S. Maria della Pace is in the fact that columns are used in the upper gallery—alternating with piers—to support an entablature as in classical temples. In quattrocento courtyards columns were made to carry arches. The cloister of S. Maria della Pace is on two levels, and in order to vary the rhythm pier is placed upon pier, but the slender columns stand over the centre of the lower arches. More spectacularly Roman, though wholly original and of his time, is the small round temple in the cloister of S. Pietro in Montorio. **187 (252-3)**

It is like one of the early Christian martyria, S. Costanza or S. Stefano Rotondo, built to contain a martyr's relics, a place of commemoration rather than worship. Architecturally it recalls the small round temple of the Sibyl at Tivoli with its peristyle and frieze.

The Tempietto presents a complete break with Bramante's Milanese style, shunning all surface ornaments, a severe, central structure on a strict ratio of proportion where height equals width in the lower and upper sections. Moreover, a circle of Doric columns, classical entablature and a parapet surround cylindrical bodies beneath a hemispherical dome. Classical metopes and triglyphs sparingly decorate the frieze. Columns fulfil their function by bearing the weight of the architrave and a projecting cornice emphasizes the roundness of the building. Shell-topped niches are hollowed out of the cylinder. In the strong southern light the columns and cupola of the Tempietto stand out in full sculptural force. By the organic relationship of its parts, the diminishing size of concentric circles, from the steps at the base to the rings of the lantern, it is a unique monument of the High Renaissance, a Pantheon in miniature. **188**

To sum up: Bramante's Tempietto, though evoked by classical models like the Temple of Vesta at Tivoli and in Rome, is not an eclectic imitation, but an autonomous rebirth. It creates a new link with Antiquity, implying a rejection as much of his own Lombard style with its jewel-like surface decoration, its sunk panels and incrustations, as of the medieval Gothic.

188. ROME. *S. Pietro in Montorio.* *Tempietto*

Small in scale, but grand in conception, the Tempietto is a wholly integrated abstract of circular horizontals, balanced by vertical continuities. It is anchored firmly to the pavement by three curving steps and a high podium. The peristyle of sixteen Doric columns with marble capitals, gently swelling organic shapes, carries the load of entablature and balusters, with doors, niches, windows in harmonious intervals of space. The drum

189. ROME. *The Vatican. The Belvedere upper courtyard (from Letarouilly)*

beneath the hemispherical dome repeats the divisions of the lower storey, of dark recesses between panelled supports, crowned by two circular bands and cornices. The geometric coherence of the structure is equally apparent in the repeated gyration of curves as in the vertical sequence of columns, triglyphs, balusters, pilasters and ribs. These shapes and lines do not contradict each other, but imperceptibly merge. In a very real sense the Tempietto is a prelude and anticipation of Bramante's un-executed plan for the new S. Peter's. It has been described as ' pure volume ' to the detriment of space, and also as pure sculpture. It fulfilled Alberti's demand that a sacred building should be isolated, domed, elevated, visible from all sides and that its decoration should not impair its structure. In that respect Bramante departed wholly from the ornate Lombard style, while the hemispherical dome was a prelude to that of S. Peter's.

For the next ten years Bramante was to design on a larger scale. Space was to be mastered in the vastness of the Belvedere Court connecting **189** the Vatican with the Belvedere villa by means of a double portico, and in the grandiose plan for S. Peter's whose walls and substructures competed with those of Imperial Rome on the Palatine hill. The colossal figure of Pope Julius set the pace. In 1506 the foundation stone was laid after the old and half ruined basilica, built by Constantine, had been demolished. Three years earlier the Belvedere Court was begun. A vast but narrow

190. ROME. *Basilica of S. Peter*

area of irregular sloping ground had to be shaped into a long terraced garden on three levels with staircase, fountain, amphitheatre and a huge exedra or half-domed niche at one end. This was flanked by a smooth wall with pairs of pilasters raised on sockets and a projecting entablature alternating with round arches set into the wall—the only surviving part of Bramante's design.

190
(202)
(203)
(234)
(241)
(242)

His original scheme for S. Peter's was accepted by Pope Julius but not completed for 120 years. It had a centralised core and a Greek-cross plan with four additional spaces around the crossing, chapels in the corners and protruding apses on all four sides. The whole space was enclosed in a huge square. Then, as now, the cylindrical drum and great hemisphere of the dome, rivalling that of the Pantheon was the outstanding feature. Bramante also planned four minor domes over the corner chapels and in the extremities four angular towers. The overall design was still the humanist's circle enclosed by a square; but now on an enormous scale. During Bramante's life only the sculptural piers beneath the dome were built and some of the walling, richly modelled like Roman walls with a new emphasis on volume. The plan still resembled Leonardo's sketches with central dome ringed by smaller satellites, yet grander and more spacious. Its centralised symmetry was changed by successive architects from Raphael to Maderno. In a sense the long history of S. Peter's is comparable to that of the Julius Tomb—the ' Tragedy of the Tomb '. For in spite of Michelangelo's sublime cupola and his gigantic encompassing of space, Bramante's original concept was transformed by the ultimate addition of a nave. But through all the vicissitudes of Mannerism and Baroque his life-giving idea remained, the soaring dome, symbolic centre of the church and the legacy of humanism.

Bramante's impact on High Renaissance architecture was as great in his followers as in his own works. His preference for centrally planned and domed churches, already evident in his early Milanese work, comes to fruition in the Roman Tempietto of S. Pietro in Montorio and reaches its fulfilment in his scheme for S. Peter's. When he became the leading architect of Pope Julius II, replanning the Vatican courts and the new S. Peter's, it was on such a scale that little was executed during his lifetime and all building was suspended at the death of Pope Julius in 1513. Yet his architectural thinking was the expression of all that the six-teenth century desired in ordered grandeur and the emulation of Imperial Rome, so that some thirty years later Michelangelo could adopt Bramante's plan for S. Peter's with only slight modifications.

In other fields, the designing of palaces, courtyards and smaller churches one must turn to the work of Bramante's collaborators, Raphael above all, Peruzzi and Antonio da Sangallo. Raphael was the heir apparent and in 1515 was appointed by Pope Leo X chief architect and surveyor of Roman antiquities. In his oeuvre architecture took second place; but Bramante's ideal of round temples had a firm hold upon him as in the crystalline beauty of the polygonal edifice, surrounded by an open arcade and raised on a flight of steps in the painting of the *Marriage of the Virgin* in the Brera Museum. This graceful temple is still of the Quattrocento but the monumental, barrel-vaulted avenues radiating in four directions from the domed centre in Raphael's *School of Athens* are a realisation in paint of Bramante's plan for S. Peter's.

Among the few buildings directed by Raphael in Rome are the immaculate Church of S. Eligio, the Chigi Chapel in S. Maria del Popolo and the elegant complex of the Villa Madama. This last, begun in 1516 191 and never completed, was terraced into the proclivities of Monte Mario, surrounded by a vast semicircular garden. Its surpassing beauty is the great loggia at the back, decorated by Giovanni da Udine and Giulio Romano with delicate stucco tracery along the radiant walls and pilasters, graceful arabesques of formalised plants and birds, urns, masks and garlands and playing children. The decoration emulates that of Nero's Golden House, especially in the richly coloured high reliefs of classical fantasies of the coffered dome, vaults and archivolts of the loggia. No more sumptuous villa exists in Rome. With its central dome supported by broad arches and pendentives, its apse-like bays, it elaborates still further the architectural idiom of Imperial Rome.

191. ROME. *Villa Madama. Loggia (photo: E.P.T. Rome)*

192. ROME. *Palazzo Vidoni Caffarelli (photo: Gabinetto Fotografico Nazionale, Rome)*

Raphael's Palazzo Vidoni Caffarelli, after a design by Bramante, **192** introduces the style of the High Renaissance to palace architecture. Here the rusticated ground floor, the alternation of pedimented windows resting on consoles, and round voussoir arches over the doorways and the pairs of fully rounded columns framing straight windows and balusters in the upper storey proclaim a new pathos and sense of power. Harmony is joined to diversity, evenness of surfacing to robustness and recession and an ordered correspondence prevails between voids and solids within the basic vocabulary of classical architecture.

P

193. ROME. *Palazzo Farnese*

The outstanding example of a High Renaissance palace in Rome came from another member of Bramante's and Raphael's circle, Antonio da Sangallo the Younger who also assisted with the work at S. Peter's. **193** Between 1534 and 1546 he built Palazzo Farnese, the most monumental of all Roman palaces where austerity and magnificence combine. The huge rectangular block of the palace is astylar, has no vertical divisions of its façade by columns or pilasters. It was completed by Michelangelo who added the widely projecting cornice, the balcony which forms the central feature, and the upper storey of the inner court. Palazzo Farnese has three long rows of windows, varied only by the shape of their pediments, triangular or segmental, supported by columns on plinths or corbels. These sculptural members stand out from the smooth walling. Elaborate string courses and the reiteration of window surrounds, emphasize the horizontal direction of the façade whose corners are strengthened by quoins. The chief ornament is Michelangelo's central window and projecting balcony over the rusticated entrance, crowned by the Farnese coat of arms, a resplendent sculptural feature in the grave monotony of the palace façade.

The square courtyard is entered through a broad, barrel-vaulted passage, resting on stout Doric columns, a magnificent gateway to the **194** interior. This is no longer a graceful Quattrocento cloister, but an arcaded quadrangle with Roman arches, supported by columns attached to piers, as in the Colosseum. On the *piano nobile* there is an Ionic order supporting

194. ROME. *Palazzo Farnese. Courtyard (photo: Gabinetto Fotografico Nazionale, Rome)*

a classical entablature and a blind arcade, encircling tabernacle windows. Above the frieze of masks and garlands Michelangelo inserted a mezzanine and a wholly original upper storey. Here superimposed pilasters are crowned by carved Corinthian capitals, and multiple consoles apparently support segmental window pediments, all Mannerist features of purely ornamental character without weight-bearing function. These segments, running close to the whimsical configuration of the upper frieze, echo the arches of the lower storeys. Thus Michelangelo's free and imaginative handling of classical motifs relieves the Roman severity of Sangallo's style.

Mannerism in Italian architecture grows imperceptibly out of the High Renaissance, forms part of it after the brief moment of the purest classical revived in the work of Bramante and Raphael, and is a long protracted phase with many facets. It is no longer a term of denigration, but rather signifies a new freedom of invention and a more fanciful use of classical motifs; or else it employs the latter as mere decoration, contravening their functional purpose. As a post-classical phenomenon it has been represented as lacking in self assurance, a protest movement and state of imbalance, related to political and religious disorders like the Sack of Rome and the Reformation. Its prime mover is Michelangelo; but the

195. ROME. *Villa Farnesina (photo: E.N.I.T. Rome)*

titanic dimensions of his genius transcend a narrow formula and his plan of S. Peter's or the re-shaping of the Capitol are the very acme of High Renaissance power in terms of shaping space and volume on the grandest scale.

Mannerism embraces the period from Baldassare Peruzzi and Giulio Romano to Vignola and Ammanati, the exaggerated Romanism of Giulio as well as the graceful scenic designs of Villa Giulia or Vignola's vastly influential façade of Il Gesù, a half-way house between Renaissance and Baroque. It is also the style which tends to break up the strict rule of the classical orders in favour of fanciful variations. It will be treated here as an integral part of the High Renaissance, not as a homogenous style, but rather as a gradual transformation of the classical vocabulary of form, now wilful, now rigid, often elegant and sophisticated.

Baldassare Peruzzi had come to Rome in 1503 from his native Siena. Like his master Bramante he began his career as a painter. His fame rests on two Roman works, the Villa Farnesina which Raphael and his pupils decorated for the banker Agostino Chigi, and on his mature masterpiece the highly unconventional Palazzo Massimi alle Colonne. The Farnesina is an early work; a central block overlooking the garden with open arcades, two superimposed rows of pilasters and a deeply carved frieze of garlands and cupids pierced by windows under the roof

195

196. ROME. *Palazzo Massimi alle Colonne*

cornice. This frieze continues along the wings projecting on either side, and the wings are also divided by pilasters. La Farnesina is a festive suburban villa, decorated with Raphael's fresco of Galathea and Giulio Romano's stories of Cupid and Psyche, an airy summer house with cunningly devised paintings of views of the Roman countryside, dissolving the reality of the walls. For Peruzzi was also a stage designer delighting in illusionist deception.

Palazzo Massimi alle Colonne was built during the last years of his **196** life (1532-36). It is no longer a square compact block with tabernacle **197** windows on columns, but fragile and insubstantial. The curved surface is explained by the bend of the road; yet it remains unique until Baroque architects made walls curve and quiver. Nor are the three orders used to scan the façade in an even rhythm. Peruzzi broke with the classical tradition of overall harmony by contrasting the ground floor portico —Doric granite columns, brightly lit against dark pools of shadow—

217

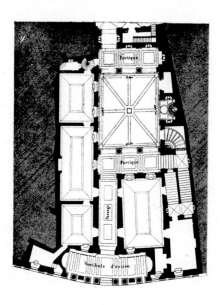

197.　Rome.　*Palazzo Massimi alle Colonne (from Letarouilly)*

with the smooth calligraphy of the upper walls and flat window surrounds. Above the *piano nobile* he placed two rows of attic windows of identical size. The handsome portico with stuccoed ceiling and Roman statues in niches is matched by the inner cortile with two orders of columns and on the first floor a sumptuously decorated loggia, giving access to the state rooms. The cortile is no less original than the façade. Here the sequence of Doric and Ionic is classical, as is the delicate frieze and entablature. But the columns are continued by small flat, vertical supports, and the intervening walls broken up by oblong openings. Among Roman palaces Palazzo Massimi alle Colonne is intimate rather than grand and, as Peruzzi was a Sienese painter and goldsmith as well as architect, and a lover of graceful and elaborate decorative mouldings, his domestic architecture is unorthodox and individual rather than mannered.

Mannerist interpretation of Bramante's and Raphael's classicism is more apparent in Giulio Romano's buildings for Frederico Gonzaga at Mantua, especially in the long low summer residence the Palazzo del **198** Tè. Here the robust facade conceals an imaginatively designed garden front with arcades supported by clustered groups of columns, boldly silhouetted against the sky. Giulio (1499—1546) was Raphael's favourite pupil, a native of Rome who after completing Raphael's legacy became the leading architect at Mantua in 1524, using motifs from Roman antiquity in an original and sometimes wilful manner.

198. MANTUA. *Palazzo del Tè.* *Detail of garden front (photo: Gabinetto Foto-grafico Nazionale, Rome)*

The Palazzo del Tè has a low frontage, rusticated throughout, whose straight windows and round arches are provided with triangular pediments and prominent keystones overlapping the string course above them. This rough surface is vertically stressed by smooth Doric pilasters, placed at irregular intervals. On the garden front the principal feature is a central atrium crowned by a classical gable, with three lofty arches supporting a coffered vault by groups of four columns carrying a heavy entablature. This sculptural feature is built in the round, but seen frontally lies flush with the wall, flanked by smaller arches on columns, and niches between pilasters. Giulio used architectural members with sublime indifference to function, now for perspective effects of view, now for pictorial alignment with the wall surface.

He even made keystones and triglyphs appear to have slipped out of place to break down the heavy monotony of the building. As a painter and decorator he was given to *trompe-l'oeil* on a grand scale, especially in the Sala dei Giganti. In Rome he had assisted Raphael in Villa Madama and in the Stanze and Loggias of the Vatican. Yet in spite of his Mannerist play and daring the overall effect of Giulio's architecture remains austerely classical, though massive and overloaded. Palazzo del Tè is essentially a summer house with a vast interior prospect of formal gardens, classical gateways and distant colonnades. Massive Doric columns and entablature, gables, arches, niches and blind arcades, firmly set into the wall of the

199. MANTUA. *House of Giulio Romano*

inner courtyard make free play with classical forms. Rough alternates
with smooth surfacing on the various façades and the complex of buildings
199 impresses by strength rather than beauty.

Giulio's own house, built in 1544 is also a one-storey palace, but
more subtle and refined with an ornamental marble frame around the
windows whose triangular pediments are recessed into arches. Plain
bands of stone set into the wall at calculated intervals and a niche sculpture
of Mercury over the depressed entrance arch enhance the elegant façade.

Michelangelo's Medici Chapel and Laurentian Library are paragons
of the Mannerist style in architecture. But this term is only applicable
to a creative genius in a revolutionary, style-transforming sense; for
Mannerism can mean academic rigidity and lifeless repetition. Rebellion
against tradition, reversal of accepted values like the classical canon of the
orders and their replacement by new dynamic forms of expression, was
Michelangelo's approach to architecture. As in painting, his language
was primarily sculptural; but contrasts between light and dark play an
important role also in his architectural designs. From 1516 onwards
Michelangelo had a share in the major building commissions of his

200. FLORENCE. *S. Lorenzo. Medici Chapel (or New Sacristy)*

age. For Pope Leo X he made a three dimensional model for the façade of S. Lorenzo with many niches to accommodate sculpture, and for Cardinal Giulio Medici, the later Clement VII, he built the Medici mausoleum (1520-34) and, in 1525, the Laurentian Library. The rebuilding of S. Peter's was the exclusive concern of the last eighteen years of his life.

The New Sacristy of S. Lorenzo was already in being when Michelangelo started his alterations to accommodate the Medici tombs and prepare the site for his sculptures. The Medici Chapel was to emulate Brunelleschi's Old Sacristy there. Michelangelo changed the size of the three bays, making the central one larger and repeating his scheme on all four sides of the room. He made the walls thicker to contain the niches for his statues and added a storey under the dome. His main concern was with the figures, the Medici princes in their recessed spaces looking across to the Madonna, and the sarcophagi below with the symbolic figures of Day and Night, Dawn and Dusk. But although he increased the central area under the great unifying arch, he did not gain more space for the effigies which were placed into narrow oblong niches and flanked by double pilasters and tabernacles. Much play has been made of the grand aedicula over the small entrance doors. These are purely ornamental and fanciful with segmental pediments and swags. In

200
(138, 139)

201. FLORENCE. *Laurenziana Library. Vestibule staircase*

contravention to classical usage their pilasters have simple block capitals·
The pediments project above the festoons and the large console brackets
beneath are like decorative scrolls.

The Medici Chapel serves as a foil for Michelangelo's sculpture.
But in the staircase vestibule of the Laurentian Library the huge paired
columns recessed into the wall have assumed the function of figurative
sculpture. Ante-room and Library must be viewed as a whole to compre-
hend the dramatic contrast between them. The vestibule with its curved
staircase cascading down from the entrance, its blind tabernacles and
large consoles ' supporting nothing ' serves as an exciting prelude to the
calm longitudinal library. Here rows of flat pilasters, framed niches and
windows articulate the walls, a perspective flight into the depth of space,
enhanced by the beams of the ceiling and the floor mosaics. The flatness
of the interior architecture in the Library contrasts strongly with the
ponderous sculptural members of the vestibule, almost wholly occupied by
the triple staircase and the ever-widening waves of steps. Moreover,
the library ceiling is low, whereas the vestibule is lofty with a high base
beneath and feigned panelling above the tabernacles whose pilasters are
tapering downwards. The shapely architectural members of the
Laurenziana are designed in a personal and compulsive style with a
sovereign disregard of the functional, in favour of the aesthetic motif.

222

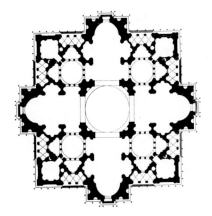

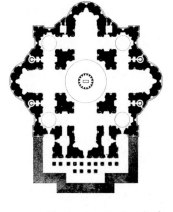

202. *Early plan of S. Peter's by Bramante (from Letarouilly)*

203. *Project for S. Peter's by Michelangelo (from Letaouilly)*

When Antonio da Sangallo died in 1546, Michelangelo took over not only as the architect of S. Peter's, but also completed the Palazzo Farnese. In S. Peter's he rejected the legacy of Raphael and Sangallo who had wanted to add a longitudinal extension to Bramante's Greek-cross church. Michelangelo adopted Bramante's central plan and by eliminating the additional spaces of the arms he concentrated on the circular core and the great cupola supported by colossal piers, already in process of being built. By shortening the arms of the cruciform plan he created a square ambulatory and conceived the dome on a truly gigantic size.

202 203 (190) (234) (241) (242)

Externally he introduced an order of Corinthian pilasters, supporting an attic storey beneath a powerful drum, with tabernacle windows between paired columns, continued by the ribs which lead up to the lantern. Michelangelo's dome of S. Peter's, completed by Giacomo della Porta in 1590, is not only a soaring monument seen from a distance, but a perfect architectural equation of thrusting and weight bearing forces, sculpturally shaped in organic growth and unity. He impressed his will and his dynamic style upon S. Peter's as we now see it, in spite of many subsequent alterations. The Gothic lengthening of the dome by Giacomo della Porta in 1590 gave to Michelangelo's (and Bramante's) hemisphere an increased upward sweep. Giacomo also added the four minor domes and ornamental detail. Even the addition of a nave and Maderno's façade (1612) could only obscure but not impair the dynamic surge of the great structure.

190

Ultimately the vast dimensions of the interior—fusion of the centralised and longitudinal plan—with the coffered and gilded tunnel vault of the nave, its four bays and colossal piers, faced by Corinthian pilasters, were to surpass all human scale. Like the Roman baths of Diocletian, massive masonry of vaults and arches and niched recesses and the great dome itself are 'boldly hollowed out as if by the sculptor's moulding hand'. The short transept and sanctuary terminate in semicircular apses—remaining core of the Greek-cross plan—and the mighty nave with its continuous cornice and entablature culminates in the central space under the cupola which is carried by piers of such magnitude as to contain in four concave niches the magniloquent statues of the full Baroque. Thus the interior of S. Peter's with all its auxiliary spaces like aisles, chapels, ambulatory is the most monumental and munificent of the High Renaissance and at the furthest remove from the intimate human scale of the Quattrocento.

This greatest Christian basilica in the West had a protracted and varied history. Its stages can now be briefly summarised. When the fabric of Old S. Peter's was crumbling, the humanist Pope Nicholas V began in 1455 to lay the foundations of a new choir zone. Half a century later the greatest patron of the arts, Pope Julius II, commissioned Bramante to build a new church over the tomb of the first apostle. A central plan was adopted in the heroic tradition of Mausolea. Bramante designed a Greek not a Latin-cross plan with a hemispherical dome after the Roman Pantheon, surrounded by four subsidiary ones over the chapels and four corner turrets. The square plan of the church formed a Greek cross by the extension of four identical apses. A square ambulatory surrounded the central dome which was raised on enormous sculptural piers. Bramante's plan for S. Peter's presented a re-thinking of his Tempietto on a grander, yet still human scale.

At the death of Bramante in 1514, when only the giant piers linking the arches were standing, Raphael took over as chief architect. To comply with the demands of the Christian ritual he designed a longitudinal nave which was never built. After his death in 1520 he was followed by Baldassare Peruzzi, another of Bramante's pupils. But in 1527 the Sack of Rome by Imperial troops interrupted all work on S. Peter's until Antonio da Sangallo became architect in charge during the 1530s. He enlarged the piers and refashioned the dome. But the greatest period of construction began only after his death in 1546 when the Farnese Pope Paul III appointed Michelangelo to the task. During the last eighteen years of his life Michelangelo set the scale for all future church building of the Counter Reformation with the overt aim to impress by superhuman grandeur. At S. Peter's the vast space under the great rotunda and cylindrical drum, the giant piers hollowed out by two-tier niches, the immense height of the dome induce a feeling of awe. Michelangelo returned to Bramante's concept and, with a dynamic force unparalleled, he eliminated the subsidiary spaces in order to concentrate on the weight-

224

bearing masonry of the piers and the vast central dome. Bramante's square plan became polygonal and later the hemisphere of the cupola was lengthened and pointed, not unlike that of Florence Cathedral.

When the death of Michelangelo occurred in 1564 the drum and attic storey of S. Peter's were completed, but the great dome itself was built by Giacomo della Porta between 1585 and 1590 from his own more ornate and upward thrusting design. He also created the minor domes over the aisles and completed Michelangelo's work on the garden side. Early in the seventeenth century the central core of the church was extended by a vast, tunnel-vaulted nave which dwarfs the aisles, hidden behind double piers and surmounted by oval cupolas. Nave and monumental façade were added by Carlo Maderno between 1607 and 1612.

Ultimately Bernini, after 1656, created the Doric colonnade around the Piazza of S. Peter's, an open forecourt or atrium to the Sanctuary. The Basilica of S. Peter's, as we see it today, is an architectural synthesis of the Renaissance, Mannerist and Baroque styles and also the triumphant expression of the classical and the Christian spirit. Among all the artists of genius working on S. Peter's, the imprint of Michelangelo remains the strongest, the most enduring.

Michelangelo's last architectural works in Rome included the conversion of part of the Baths of Diocletian into the church of S. Maria degli Angeli, and in a much lighter vein, the Porta Pia (1562) a gateway which formed the terminus of a long and straight avenue. Although originally part of the city wall, its thinness of texture and decorative nature precludes a defensive character at a time when Sanmicheli in Verona was building his fortress-like Porta Pallio with solid, rusticated walls and Doric columns. Even the battlements of Michelangelo's city gate are made to carry ornamental spheres and there are many elements of a bizarre and proto-Baroque character such as broken pediments, curvilinear scrolls and volutes, fluted pilasters and garlands. Porta Pia is designed for the painterly effect of strong light and shadow. Structural tension and domination of mass have been abandoned in favour of scenic effects. It is Michelangelo's ultimate rejection of *Romanità*, preparing the way for the end-phase of the Renaissance in the architecture of the Roman Baroque.

Michelangelo's influence on his immediate successors like Giacomo della Porta and on the architects of the seventeenth century like Bernini was incalculable. Architecture, like its sister arts, has a human connotation, especially in antiquity and the Renaissance. But Michelangelo broke away from the human measure by his preference for the immense, the giant orders, the colossal dome. He substituted the static calm of the Renaissance by a baroque sense of movement. Already in 1888 the

204. ROME. *Porta Pia (photo: E.N.I.T. Rome)*

Swiss historian Wölfflin demonstrated this change, contrasting the sharply defined and individualised shapes of the Renaissance with the opulent, rounded and massive forms of the Baroque. Movement and convexity were evident in the Laurentian staircase. Columns were 'imprisoned' in the wall, just as some of Michelangelo's sculptures were embedded in the marble block from which they struggle in vain to free themselves. Style in architecture admits of human interpretation.

The Laurenziana appeared to Wölfflin to be lacking in a sense of fulfilment or necessity, qualities which we now associate with Mannerism. He perceived a violent struggle between form and mass and a perpetual movement. In the Palazzo dei Conservatori the sheer weight of the upper storey seemed to press the columns below against the giant piers. At S. Peter's all considerations of human scale and comfort were abandoned in favour of a craving for the colossal. This was accompanied externally

226

205. ROME. *S. Andrea in Via Flaminia (photo: Gabinetto Fotografico Nazionale, Rome)*

206. ROME. *Il Gesù* (*photo: E.N.I.T. Rome*)

by the broad Corinthian pilasters and the insertion of a large attic storey
with strangely cut windows and niches as a mighty base for drum and
dome. Most other cupolas in Rome and more especially that of Il Gesù
and the articulation of its façade depend on Michelangelo's work at S.
Peter's.

The leading architects in Rome beside and after Michelangelo were
Vignola and Giacomo della Porta. The more original of the two is
Vignola who launched out in new directions, whereas Giacomo completed
and modified Michelangelo's work on the Capitol Hill and in S. Peter's.

228

207. ROME. *Il Gesù (photo: E.N.I.T. Rome)*

He also continued the building of Vignola's masterpiece, the church of Il Gesù, changing the design of its façade. But it was Vignola who evolved step by step the new type of church of the Counter-Reformation, combining a longitudinal with a central plan, an aisleless nave with a light-giving dome. He abandoned the circular plan of the Renaissance and its self-sufficient unity by lengthening the ground plan, creating a rectangular nave with an oval dome above. This he did in the small oratory of S. Andrea in Via Flaminia, combining the cube with the **205** cylinder. Hence it was only logical to raise an oval dome over an elliptical

Q

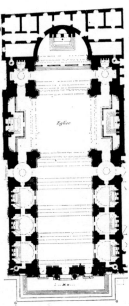

208. ROME. *Il Gesù* (*from Letarouilly*)

ground plan and this became the preferred shape of Bernini and Borromini in their most sophisticated creations of the Roman Baroque, S. Andrea al Quirinale and S. Carlo alle Quattro Fontane.

206-208

Vignola's design for Il Gesù commissioned in 1568 by the Jesuit Order, set the pattern for the churches of the Counter-Reformation and was prefigured by Alberti's interior of S. Andrea at Mantua. The lengthening of the central axis in the main body of the church produced a longitudinal plan but with a new emphasis on movement towards the simulated heaven of the dome from whose windows great shafts of light are flooding the church. With this focal centre, an extended nave and short barrel-vaulted transepts and apse, Il Gesù has no aisles, only dark side-chapels, opening onto the nave as in Alberti's S. Andrea at Mantua. The majestic dome is supported at the crossing by four triumphal arches on giant piers and pendentives, forming part of the massive wall structure. Great projecting cornices above the pilasters of the nave emphasize the horizontal sweep by which the worshippers are compelled towards the central space. Externally Vignola's façade had a Renaissance sobriety of well-defined forms, two storeys, like S. Maria Novella, with a gabled top and descending scrolls, an entrance arch framed by columns, and double pilasters enclosing niches and porches. Giacomo della Porta's alterations gave the façade of Il Gesù a heavier, more massive shape. The super-

209. ROME. *Villa di Papa Giulio. Courtyard (photo: E.N.I.T. Rome)*

structure is broader, the scrolls more curling, cornice and attic are enlarged. The lower part has plain panels and heavy bases for columns and pilasters. Decorative members like pediments, consoles, colonettes and balusters speak the Mannerist idiom of Michelangelo.

Vignola was the most influential and versatile architect during the later stages of the Renaissance in Rome. For besides creating the archetypal form of Jesuit churches, consisting of a large aisleless nave with side chapels for saying mass, a dome over the crossing and spacious transepts—he also designed sumptuous villas and pleasure gardens in and outside Rome. Together with Vasari and Ammanati he built the Villa di Papa Giulio, a country house with extended views through a 209-211 sequence of semicircular courtyard, loggia and colonnade towards a walled garden. It is a scenic design of extreme elegance with fanciful variations of the classical orders, especially in the Nymphaeum where sculptured herms are used as supports in lieu of columns. This villa suburbana, built between 1550-55 for the pleasure loving Julius III is the most stylish in Italy, vieing with the villas of Imperial Rome, especially in the great hemispherical colonnade, supporting a straight entablature, which surrounds the inner court. A triple portico, recessed within a screening wall, leads to the Nymphaeum and hence to the secret garden. The most delicately shaped Nymphaeum, lying at a lower level with shaded recesses, mosaic pavement and the exhilarating run of its balusters is a disciplined fusion of straight and curvilinear forms. The elaborate garden façade of

210. ROME. *Villa di Papa Giulio. Nymphaeum (photo: E.P.T. Roma)*

Villa Giulia, concealed behind the block-like street front and rusticated triumphal arch, and the transition from villa to court, from court to garden, embellished by classical sculptures, arcades and porticoes create an ample as well as an intimate domain for gracious living.

Besides cooperating with Vignola at Villa Giulia, Ammanati built Ponte S. Trinità, the finest Florentine bridge over the Arno and also the garden façade of Palazzo Pitti. Ammanati's Mannerist courtyard of 1568 is more sculptural than linearistic on account of the cyclopic blocks of varying size and form which compose the Doric, Ionian and Corinthian orders. These squares or rounded shapes, placed with great freedom, parallel or oblique, are on a colossal scale. The Renaissance simplicity and equipoise of the façade has been maintained in the added wings and annexes of the palace, but the ponderous and projecting members of the cortile and their pictorial effects of light and shadow anticipate the Baroque.

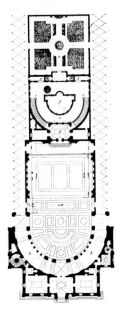

211. ROME. *Villa di
Papa Giulio (from
Letarouilly)*

Vignola's Villa Farnese at Caprarola is a palace in the country, **213**
not a villa but a large seigneurial mansion originally planned as a fortress
on a hill-top dominating the Farnese estate. Vignola converted it into
the most spectacular architectural garden complex of the Renaissance.
The pentagonal palace is reached by a sequence of curvilinear and rectangular ramps with flights of stairs and balusters rising from terrace to
terrace to the threshold of the building. The porches are rusticated in
contrast to the smooth walling of the palace. The projecting bastions
are linked by their cornices to the *piano nobile*. Here flat pilasters separate
large round-headed windows, whereas the upper storey has small oblong
windows, topped by a mezzanine, increasing the height of the palace.
The end bays are strengthened by quoins. The famous circular courtyard, inscribed within the pentagon, has paired Ionian half-columns
and round arches in the style of Bramante, enclosing narrow bays with
rectangular openings or niches. This double row of arcades draws its
strength from the triumphal arch motif and the rustication at ground
level. The pentagonal form of the fortress villa dominating the countryside, determined the layout of the extensive gardens which Vignola
designed in the shape of two main rectangles, overlooked from two
sides of the palace; a vast geometrical complex of terraces, bounded by

212. FLORENCE. *Palazzo Pitti. Garden façade* (*photo: E.P.T. Florence*)

213. CAPRAROLA. *Villa Farnese*

214. ROME. *Palazzo Spada* (*photo: E.P.T. Rome*)

walls and copses, with stone walks, fountains and garden sculpture on
a lavish scale and an airy pavilion which is Vignola's finest creation.
Caprarola is the grandest of Italian gardens of the Renaissance, designed
for the festive life of a Roman Prince of the Church.

Cardinal del Monte, on the eve of his becoming Pope Julius III,
built himself one of the most decorative palaces in Rome, later acquired
by Cardinal Spada which, on account of its profusion of stucchi on the
façade and in the courtyard, has been ascribed to Giulio Mazzoni. Palazzo
Spada (begun in 1550), is remarkable for the contrast between a high,
rusticated basement, laid in alternating courses, and a first storey which
in its fantastic richness of ornament and pictorialism—dark window
recesses side by side with gesturing figures in niches—is already proto-
baroque. These are the heroes of ancient Rome like Romulus and
Caesar, Augustus and Trajanus whose names and deeds are inscribed
in large tablets under the roof cornice. The portal, built of irregular
blocks and voussoirs, projects slightly and is topped by a large crest and
crown in the piano nobile. Here oval medallions, candelabra, festoons,
Victories and putti, holding garlands or unfurled banners, compose a
continuous frieze. Even the niches are crowned by triangular pediments
and the whole wall surface blossoms out in sculptural relief. This is
repeated to even finer effect in the Grand Courtyard; for here the solid

235

215. ROME. *Palazzo Spada. Second courtyard*

base is broken up into large arcades whose dark interior counteracts the wealth of figures and friezes above. A second courtyard is reached through a short passage where, by a feat of perspective illusionism, Borromini has suggested a long colonnade. In spite of its block-like structure Palazzo Spada has a playful and festive appearance, exceptional in sixteenth century Rome, and on this account, is another form of Mannerist experiment, a Rococo fantasy *avanti la lettera*.

In its more extreme forms Mannerist architecture is pictorial rather than structural. The façades of Palazzo Spada and of Villa Pia in the Vatican Gardens are overlaid with ornamental motifs. The latter was built by Pirro Ligorio between 1558 and 1564. Here the Vitruvian orders are almost obliterated by sunk panels in high relief dividing the façade in separate units. Carved swags and garlands abound and even the crowning pediment is ornamented. The festive frontage of Villa Pia

216. MILAN. *Palazzo Marino.* *Second courtyard* (*photo: Gabinetto Fotografico Nazionale, Rome*)

resembles a stage set rather than a three dimensional building. The Doric columns of the portico are the only classical feature; but in the upper storey the orders are replaced by human caryatides at the corners, by spiral colonettes enframing figures, and vertical panels loaded with swags of fruit in lieu of pilasters. Another famous example of decorative relief sculpture taking over from the classical orders is the inner courtyard of Palazzo Marino in Milan where arcades supported by twin columns are **216** the only structural members amidst a profusion of carved panels, herms and lion head consoles, niche figures on huge pedestals and friezes with swags. Galeazzo Alessi, the architect was inspired by a proto-Baroque *horror vacui*. Born in Perugia (1512-72) and trained in Michelangelo's Rome, he became the chief architect of High Renaissance villas and palaces in Genoa. Palazzo Marino is his last and extravagantly Mannerist work.

Michelangelo himself treated architectural forms for decorative purposes in sovereign disregard of their weight-bearing function. He conceived the stairway, columns, consoles or pediments as sculptural elements or empty niches and flat frames as pure *disegno* and wall ornaments. But Michelangelo was a Mannerist of genius, and his interior architecture, though irrational, has a stylistic force and coherence which raises it to the level of great art.

217. FLORENCE. *Uffizi, looking towards the Arno*

This is not the case in the work of his friend and follower Vasari, whose one outstanding architectural achievement—the Uffizi—is a piece of town planning, a narrow channel of a street, flanked by two lofty palace wings between Piazza della Signoria and the river Arno. Vasari blends a number of classical forms like Doric columns and entablature, interrupted by piers and niche-sculpture in a three-bay rhythm, corresponding with the windows above. The two wings of the building are linked at the end by an airy archway and large 'Serlian windows' to provide a contrast of light to the dark gallery of the long and narrow

218. VERONA. *Bevilacqua Palace*

street. Pilaster stips, consoles and square frames overlay the walls to no functional purpose. But the triumphal arch at the riverside has lightness and elegance, recalling Vignola's Villa Giulia where Vasari was co-architect.

Surprise is another element of Mannerist architecture, a straight façade concealing a semi-circular inner court or an unexpected sequence of garden vistas seen through arches and porticoes (Palazzo del Tè, Villa Giulia). The classical orders are used with great freedom and variation of shape, scale and grouping. At its best the Mannerist style produces fragile and elegant scenographic structures suited for villas and garden architecture or else it debases antique forms in an overloaded

219. VENICE. *Palazzo Corner della Cà Grande (Prefettura)*

manner to convey strength. It is squat and heavy in Giulio Romano, rebellious in regard to the classical past in Michelangelo, light-hearted and exquisite in Vignola or decorative in Pirro Ligorio, Alessi and Sanmicheli. A notable example of the last is Palazzo Bevilacqua in Verona.

Here the classical orders have been strangely transformed: rusticated block pilasters below and spiral columns alternating with fluted ones above. The wall of the piano nobile is almost totally taken over by the windows, large bays alternating with small, wide with narrow, and the spandrels are filled with ornamental sculpture of Victories and River Gods. Even the keystones at the window tops are figurative, busts of emperors, lion heads and garlands. A continuous balcony runs along the lower cornice, supported by brackets which are really projecting triglyphs of the Doric entablature. The entrance to the palace has been placed perversely not in the centre of the building but in a second bay. To complete the decoration a frieze of foliage and sirens runs below the large overhang of the roof. The 'massive muscularity' of Palazzo Bevilacqua is stressed by pictorial effects of light and shade which throw sculptural forms, columns, balconies, keystones into strong relief, heralding Sansovino's masterpiece, the Libreria Vecchia in Venice. Thus Mannerism in Italian architecture is a generic term, embracing many experimental styles of the Late Renaissance, it can hardly be said to anticipate the Baroque, but elaborates and sometimes abuses the vocabulary of classicism.

Venetian architecture, conditioned by Byzantine and Gothic influences and by the Lombard genius for geometrical pattern and decoration owes its unity to the painterly effects of sun, air and sea. The style of the High Renaissance in Venice was not a native growth. It came through the mediation of one man, a native of Florence, but educated in the Rome of Bramante, Raphael and Michelangelo: Jacopo Tatti, called Sansovino. Sculptor as well as architect, he had settled in Venice after the Sack of Rome in 1527 and within two years rose to be protomagister of S. Marco. He exerted the greatest influence upon the urban image of Venice before the coming of Palladio.

In palace architecture and statuary, but chiefly by the superb horizontal sweep of double arcading in the Libreria Vecchia, facing the Ducal Palace, he left his mark upon the city of his adoption. The impact of the Roman Renaissance upon the Venetian tradition is strongest in Sansovino's Palazzo Corner della Cà Grande, on the Canale Grande. **219** The monumental palace is boldly and safely poised on the water's edge with its strong rusticated ground floor and three high central porches which overshadow the small window bays on either side. Over this powerful base Sansovino built two identical upper storeys with paired columns of the Ionian and Corinthian order, separating arched windows, and a balcony uniting the three central bays. Columns, cornices and keystones are not only sculptural features, but—like the ground floor arcades—adapt the Roman style to the Venetian play of light and shadow, of alternating voids and solids. There is nothing tentative about Palazzo Corner, rising squarely in three-dimensional robustness on the Venetian lagoon. Yet if the confident Roman palace does not seem quite at home among the Byzantine and Gothic buildings lining the canal, Jacopo's

220. VENICE. *Libreria Vecchia, detail*

Libreria Vecchia, continued by the Loggetta at the base of the Campanile was a solution of genius to the problem of harmonizing the old with the new. For in 1537 he was commissioned with the greatest urbanistic task of the century, that of building the Marcian Library on the Piazzetta opposite the Doge's palace, the Loggetta, facing S. Marco's and the Mint adjoining the Library on the waterfront. The fate of the most

221. VENICE. *La Zecca (the Mint) (photo: Alinari/E.P.T. Venice)*

beautiful piazza in the world depended on his matching without obliterating the beauty of the existing buildings. To balance the Gothic arcades
and the long pink frontage of Palazzo Ducale with its rhythmic intervals
of window openings and the impeccable proportions of the whole seemed
an impossible undertaking.

Sansovino designed the Library lower than the Doge's palace, but
enriched it with sculptural ornament placing a figure above each pier.
He made no attempt at emulating the impeccable planar surface or the
exquisite lacework arcading of Palazzo Ducale, but boldly designed a
double order of loggias with Doric columns below, Ionic above and
a continuous frieze and balcony running the whole length of the façade.
The classical entablature of metopes and triglyphs formed a tangent to
the arches below, with heads of men and of lions serving as keystones.
The upper frieze is more richly carved with heavy garlands and putti
alternating with oculi openings. Stylistically the Old Library offers no
parallel to the Doge's Palace except for the painterly effects of light and
shadow; but these are obtained by opposing radiant sculptural forms,
columns, friezes, balconies and statues to the dark recesses of loggias

222. MASER (Treviso). *Villa Barbaro* (*now Volpi*)

and windows with no solid walling left in the structure. The Loggetta beneath the Campanile continues the decorative façade of the Library on a lighter scale, using its elements and divisions more gracefully with elegant classical figures placed in niches between the slender colonettes, a tripartite division of arches and corresponding relief panels above the cornice. Sculpture and architecture appear wholly integrated. The Mint (La Zecca) adjoining the Library on the water front has no stylistic relation to it. Rusticated arches below and banded columns abvoe and an uncommonly heavy entablature give the impression of a stronghold rather than a civic building.

Evolution in continuity signifies the syncretistic art of Venice, where styles of different ages and civilisations meet in harmony. Titian and Sansovino alone represent the High Renaissance in Venice. Their near contemporaries typify either a highly personal and expressionist mannerism with a Byzantine flavour like Tintoretto or a new classical serenity and opulence like Veronese and in a sense Palladio.

Andrea Palladio is the most universally known of Italian architects and the most imitated. Moreover, he is wholly Venetian, grown and bred outside the Renaissance centres of Florence and Rome. Born in Padua, he began as a stone mason, but was fortunate in finding an erudite patron in Count Trissino, humanist, poet and dilettante-architect who employed and trained him in classical architecture and theory and introduced him to Rome. Palladio's work was confined to the Veneto and more

221

244

especially to the area of Vicenza, Padua and Venice. By his public buildings and palaces he remodelled the townscape of Vicenza. Other than Michelangelo or Jacopo Sansovino he remained a pure architect all his life without practising painting or sculpture. His most intimate art form is the country villa, his most monumental the two churches which dominate the skyline of Venice. He also wrote an important treatise on architecture, the *Quattro Libri*. Endowed with a sense for mathematical proportions and harmony and schooled in Vitruvius, he was an intellectual artist who created cubic spaces and geometrical divisions of wall surfaces. Perhaps he arrived at his most significant forms in the patrician villas, some distinctly rural, consisting of a main residential block, continued on both sides by recessed wings or arcades to serve as outbuildings or storage rooms—and in the suburban villas comparable to those of the Medici in Poggio a Caiano, Careggi or Fiesole.

Palladio's Villa Barbaro at Maser belongs to the rustic type. It is **222** one of the finest on account of its relaxed nobility and poise, its long and radiant frontage, fusing imperceptibly with the wooded hillside behind. Villa Barbaro has a central two-storey block with an ornamented pediment and four attached columns. The extensive arcades are set back in space, coming forward again at the ends where concave gables echo the straight ones of the main villa. It is a Venetian Sanssouci built for two scholars and dignitaries of the Venetian republic. The chief glory within are Veronese's frescoes of allegorical scenes and figures, feigned architecture and landscape vistas connecting the internal space with surrounding nature and using Palladio's forms in the illusionist arches and balusters. All the three arts co-operate; for on the façade and on the keystones Vittoria carved stuccoed masks and mythological figures and his statues line the approaches to the house.

In most of his villas Palladio adopted the cubic block and temple front as his preferred shape, projecting, recessed or aligned with the wings of the building and approached by a flight of stairs. Some of the villas have a double portico on two levels and two storeys like Villa Cornaro and Villa Pisani. In Villa Foscari (La Malcontenta) one order **223** of Ionic columns supporting entablature and gable is set on an uncommonly high base, and here the external symmetry mirrors the interior harmony of well-proportioned rooms around an all but square central hall two storeys high. La Rotonda is also basically a cube, but crowned and lit **224** by a shallow dome. It is a more complex structure, repeating the projecting temple-front and flight of stairs on all four sides. The classical serenity of Palladio's villas is arrived at by simple geometry and an innate sense of dignity and measure. The architectural parts are derived from antiquity, but purified by simple processes of rationalisation. These

245

R

223. MESTRE. *Villa Malcontenta (Villa Foscari)*

villas were designed for Venetian and Vicentine noblemen as places of repose and retreats from a busy life of affairs.

Palladio's palaces and civic buildings in Vicenza, ten in number, are clearly of two kinds: street palaces in the tradition of Bramante, Raphael and Giulio Romano, and public buildings surrounding squares to be approached from a distance. Examples of the former are Palazzo Porto, Thiene and Valmarana, following a Renaissance-cum-Mannerist pattern, rusticated ground floor with voussoir arches over the windows and in the first floor pedimented windows between engaged columns above which the entablature comes forward; also some sculptural ornament, figures, garlands and male heads for keystones (Palazzo Iseppe Porto). In Palazzo Thiene the heavy rustication of the basement is taken up by the window jambs in contrast to the smooth walling and flat pilasters of the *piano nobile* and the repeated emphasis on a horizontal division of the façade. This is Palladio's closest approximation to Giulio Romano.

246

224. VICENZA. *La Rotonda*

In Palazzo Valmarana the giant order of Michelangelo's Capitol buildings is translated into two-storey pilasters, rising from a solid base. There are reliefs above the ground floor windows and in the pendentives of the entrance arch. **225**

Palladio's public buildings in Vicenza are more spectacular. The earliest is the Basilica or town hall (1545), followed by Palazzo Chiericati (1550) and the Loggia del Capitano (1572). In the Basilica Palladio gave to a medieval building a double portico of Imperial Roman character, but with a new emphasis on the pictorial contrasts of light and shadow within the wide Roman archways, the heavy engaged columns with projecting entablature and the smaller recessed order. The columns are Doric below, Ionic above. The balconies, sculptures and heavy twin-columned piers at the corners increase the effects of colour and light of the majestic Basilica. **226**

By contrast, Palazzo Chiericati is more airy and elegant. Here the central block slightly projects from the colonnaded wings. Sculpted figures on the segmental window pediments recall Michelangelo's sarcophagi in the Medici Chapel. Though the elements are Roman, the character of Palazzo Chiericati has acquired Vicentine birth-right by a transformation **227**

247

225. VICENZA. *Palazzo Valmarana* (*photo: E.P.T. Vicenza*)

226. VICENZA. *The Basilica*

of these elements into a native style: the double columns stressing the central part, the tripartite division of the façade, the continuous entablature and balustrade, triangular and segmental pediments alternating over the windows and lastly the elevated and isolated positioning of the palace. The Loggia del Capitano, a late work, is really a triumphal arch heavily ornamented with swags and sculpture. In the last year of his life Palladio built the Teatro Olimpico, completed by his pupil Scamozzi, with a permanent *trompe-l'oeil* stage-set and a huge semicircular auditorium in the style of a Roman arena.

Apart from the circular chapel of Villa Maser, a separate building combining central plan, Greek-cross design and a temple front with a decorative profusion of delicate stuccoes which herald the eighteenth century—Palladio's church buildings are all in Venice: the façade of S. Francesco della Vigna and the two landmarks on the Venetian skyline—Il Redentore and S. Giorgio Maggiore. In church and palace architecture the Venetian tradition was pre-eminently Gothic and Byzantine. Pietro Lombardo and Mauro Coducci introduced the Quattrocento, Palladio the High Renaissance style to ecclesiastial buildings. S. Maria dei Miracoli, S. Zaccaria and the Scuola di S. Marco merge imperceptibly with the squares and waterways of Venice. Palladio's churches with their domes, bell towers and temple fronts are a new urbanistic feature, as were his civic buildings, villas and palaces in the Veneto.

228

249

227. VICENZA. *Palazzo Chiericati*

First in time was the façade of S. Francesco della Vigna which Palladio built in 1562 to screen the body of Sansovino's church. It has all the criteria of his subsequent church façades: a large order of four engaged columns crowned by a pediment to indicate the nave, and flanked by a smaller order with triangular half-pediments corresponding with aisles or side chapels. The temple fronts are more complex than the porticoes of Palladio's villas.

In S. Giorgio Maggiore (1566 ff.) and Il Redentore (1576 ff.) on the Giudecca, Palladio devised plans comparable to Vignola's Il Gesù, fusing a Latin cross with a central, domed space, short transepts and rounded apse. S. Giorgio has open arched aisles supported on giant

228. VICENZA. *Loggia del Capitano*

229. VENICE. *S. Francesco della Vigna (photo: Alinari/E.P.T. Venice)*

230. VENICE. *S. Giorgio Maggiore*

231. VENICE. *Il Redentore (from J. Gailhabaud, Monuments)*

232. Venice. *Il Redentore* (*photo: Alinari/E.P.T. Venice*)

piers, but Il Redentore dispenses with aisles for side chapels joined by a passage. In both Venetian churches Palladio adapted the Byzantine dome and the massive moulded vaults of the Imperial baths and the pedimented columnar templefront of Rome to the Venetian ambience. The façades are of marble and employ the same orders as the interior. In S. Giorgio **230** the columns are set on a high base, whereas the pilasters start from ground level. In the more accomplished Redentore there are no pedestals. The **231** façade is articulated by three pediments: one over the porch, recessed half-pediments over the chapels and a third one embracing the giant order beneath the square attic storey. The distinctive feature of the interior is the semicircular screen of columns which separates the brightly **232** lit choir from the main body of the church. Thus a mystical element is added to the logic of architectural spaces which draws the visitor from the barrel vaulted nave towards the expanding area of dome and crossing with the monastic choir beyond and its undefined space. Light is also reflected from the bright stucco surfaces clothing the brick walling. In spite of the Roman austerity of the orders and the symmetry of temple façades, S. Giorgio Maggiore and Il Redentore are wholly integrated into the Venetian cityscape. The shadowless whiteness of marble fronts blends well with the warm brick walls, and the geometrical shapes of architectural members unite with the Byzantine dome and surging spire. By his majestic forms and calculated proportions and sparing ornaments Palladio imparted new life to the traditional language of classical architecture.

Moreover, learned archaeologist and scholar that he was, Palladio conducted a 'belated Renaissance' in the Veneto. In church and palace architecture the determining factor for him was the classical orders, be it the free standing columns and weighty entablatures in Il Redentore or the open colonnades of Palazzo Chiericati, where only the central section of the upper storey is given over to solid walls, enclosing a great hall. Thus Palladio with his vast knowledge of classical forms and proportions transferred the Latin language of architecture and the sculptural definition of the orders to his Vicentine and Venetian buildings and exacted a decisive influence upon eighteenth century architecture in England.

CHAPTER SIX

THE ARCHITECTURE OF THE BAROQUE 1600-1750

Maderno — Bernini — Borromini — Cortona — Longhena — Guarini — Juvarra
Baroque architecture in Italy is more than a postlude to the Renaissance. In a sense
it is its summary, its fulfilment. Though Guarini and Borromini were daring innovators
using static walls for dynamic and undulating movement—just as Bernini gave to
sculpture a new vitality and dimension or Cortona to fresco painting. Nonetheless they
all carried the classical tradition with them into the seventeenth century, however
modified or disguised. All employed the classical orders and upheld the Renaissance
ideal of the centrally planned church as the most perfect form of the Christian temple.
Once a derogatory term, the Baroque is now recognized as a vital enlargement of
architectural form and of the aesthetic experience. To take its measure one need
only mention Bernini's universally famed colonnade of S. Peter's or the great
palaces like Palazzo Barberini in Rome, or Palazzo Pesaro in Venice, or the cerem-
onial staircases, the fantastic fountains or architectural gardens. But it is in
ecclesiastical buildings that the Baroque, the style of the Counter-Reformation had
its greatest triumphs, be it in the grandiloquent facade of S. Peter's, the many domed
churches of Rome, or S. Maria della Salute in Venice shapely and monumental,
the superb mountain sanctuary of La Superga near Turin or the more intimate and
sophisticated oval space-creations of S. Carlino or S. Andrea in Rome which are the
quintessence of the Italian Baroque and of great consequence for the dissemination
of the style in Southern Europe.

After Giacomo della Porta's death in 1602 it fell to a powerful architect
from the north to take charge of the work at S. Peter's. He was Carlo
Maderno, born near Lugano in 1556 who had come to Rome in 1588 to
assist his uncle Domenico Fontana. By 1603 he had already achieved his
masterpiece, the façade of S. Susanna. This depended from Vignola's Il
Gesù, but with a difference; for, whereas the frontage of the Gesù was
smooth and staid, S. Susanna had sculptural and dynamic qualities and   **233**
vertical rather than horizontal stresses. Composed in two tiers with
massive volutes and a triangular pediment, its decorative crescendo worked
inwards from the outer bays with their pilasters and flat frames containing
festoons, towards the rounded columns, deep niches with full-length figures
and richly ornamented doorway. In the upper storey double pilasters
echo the twin columns below; here the sculptured tabernacles have
semicircular or broken pediments. The diminishing volume of the
vertical orders and the concentration on the central structure convey an
impulsive movement.

A central doorway framed by twin columns and crowned by a
gable is also the basic shape of Maderno's portico of S. Peter's. He   **234**
completed the façade in 1614, screening the whole width of the building,   **(190)**
including choir and transepts, and for this purpose Maderno built two   **(202)**

233. ROME. *S. Susanna (photo: E.N.I.T. Rome)*

(203)
(241)
(242) outer bays with two campanili. The latter were never completed and finally demolished in 1646. Maderno's scope was restricted not only by the existing proportions of the façade, but also by the necessity of building the Loggia of Benediction. To restore the balance between length and height he designed the two end-towers, but these would have impaired the effect of Michelangelo's cupola. Moreover, by changing Bramante's and Michelangelo's Greek-cross plan into a Latin cross, he

258

234. ROME. *Basilica of S. Peter, Maderno's portico*

235. ROME. *Dome of S. Andrea della Valle*

obscured the external view of the cupola which is set back in space. The longitudinal nave prevents the visitor entering the basilica from realizing the great circular void over the crossing before he stands under Michelangelo's dome.

235
236
    In S. Andrea della Valle, Maderno was to create the largest and most beautiful cupola in Rome after S. Peter's. The interior of the church followed the prototype of Il Gesù—a broad single nave with lateral chapels—and the dome depended on Michelangelo's. It rises on an octagonal drum whose facets are separated by twin columns with Ionian capitals under a projecting cornice. These columns are continued

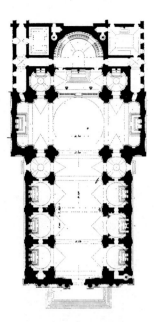

236. ROME. *S. Andrea della Valle* (*from Letarouilly*)

by eight ribs which terminate in an elegant lantern scanned by twin colonettes. The floating nature and a certain weightlessness of the dome are aided by the flatness of the ribs and the semi-elliptical shape with small windows and oculi. The half-columns of the drum, framing large pedimented windows, are crowned by protruding and retreating cornices so that an undulating horizontal movement balances the upward sweep. In its clear divisions and fully integrated individual sections and members, Maderno's cupola is of compelling structural logic and aesthetic beauty.

In domestic architecture Maderno also made his mark upon Rome during the transition period to the vigorous full Baroque. His Palazzo Barberini is the first grandiloquent Baroque palace in Rome. **237**

Planned as a huge block with four sides of nineteen bays and an inner courtyard, the latter was replaced by a three-sided atrium. The palace was completed by Giovanni Lorenzo Bernini and its three-storeyed façade has been attributed to him. Yet this resplendent façade with its open arcade and seven large, roundheaded windows and a receding end-bay on either side, linking the wings to the centre, may well be after Maderno's design. The three orders of the façade follow the classical sequence of the Doric, Ionian and Corinthian style. The sculptural quality of half-columns in the second storey is diminished by applied

261

237. ROME. *Palazzo Barberini*

pilasters in the third, the same diminuendo as in the façade of S. Susanna. The upper windows have illusionist arches, feigning a perspective recession in space, a painterly device of the proto-Baroque. In the following of Michelangelo, but never his imitator, Maderno's work forms a bridge between the final stages of the Renaissance and the incipient Baroque. His ecclesiastic and domestic architecture shows him as a master of monumental substance, dynamic force and varied invention.

Paradoxical as it may seem, Bernini is the last universal genius of the Renaissance as well as the leading artist of the Baroque. His architecture

238. Ariccia (Rome). *S. Maria dell'Assunzione*

is a concomitant of his exuberant sculpture, although he came to it late in life and made it subservient to the latter. He transformed the urban image of Rome by his work for S. Peter's, the famous colonnade, the great fountains, the figures on the Ponte S. Angelo, the architectural baldacchino within the Basilica, the Cornaro Chapel, the Scala Regia, the palaces, the churches. Bernini's church architecture, apart from S. Peter's is structurally restrained, classicist, severe and entirely based on geometrical bodies: cylinder, hemisphere and oval and on the pedimented portico inherited from Palladio. One would hardly expect to find Palladian shapes in the undisputed leader of the Roman Baroque, the rival of Borromini, the friend and servant of four popes and the artistic dictator of the Counter-Reformation in its later stages.

His first essay in architecture was a most conservative building, the church of S. Bibiana, commissioned by Pope Urban VIII on his accession

263

239. ROME. *S. Andrea al Quirinale* (*photo: E.N.I.T. Rome*)

in 1624. It consists of square, block-like forms, a round-arched portico and applied pilasters. Its main feature is a projecting centre bay and triangular superstructure which continues the giant order into the second storey and towers above the wings of the church. But Bernini's more original creations stem from the 1660s and are at Castelgandolfo, Ariccia and, the climax of them all, S. Andrea al Quirinale. They are centrally planned churches with domes and coffered vaulting.

At Castelgandolfo the dome is raised on a drum, but in Ariccia it rises straight from a circular cornice, a pure hemisphere like the Roman Pantheon. Both cupolas are coffered with elegant ribs, filled with light and decorated with garland-holding angels. At Castelgandolfo, the chapel of the papal summer seat, they are placed above the windows of the drum on broken pediments, holding large medallions, as well as being linked by festoons across the base of the ribs. But at Ariccia there

240. ROME. *S. Andrea al Quirinale. Inside of cupola*

is no intervening drum between the great circular cornice and the dome, and here the angels sit on volutes, holding wreathes to crown the Virgin, for this is the church of the Assumption. Externally S. Maria del l'Assunzione is composed of a perfect cylinder capped by a hemisphere and preceded by a triangular portico, geometrical shapes so basic and so unadorned as to present an organic whole. A severe and symmetrical classicism reigns, even in the three chapels facing each other on either side of the central axis which is formed by the entrance portico opposite the altar recess. Moreover, the rotundity of the building is enhanced by the rectangular walls and piers surrounding it.

But the most exhilarating solution for a small church is Bernini's S. Andrea al Quirinale, built between 1658 and 1670, the church of the Jesuit Noviciate. It is with Borromini's S. Carlo alle Quattro Fontane the supreme achievement of the Baroque style. Here Bernini replaced

239

the sphere by the oval and oriented his interior space along the transversal axis according to the elliptical shape of the plan, where the distance between entrance and altar is the shorter of the two. Giant pilasters scan the walls around the nave supporting a curvilinear cornice. Above the windows and ribs of the coffered vault, rising towards the lantern in the radiant light, cherubs and the Dove of the Holy Ghost suggest the heavenly sphere. For this is the church of S. Andrew and his figure soaring upon clouds, breaks through the semicircular pediment above the sanctuary. Here the four Corinthian columns screen the tabernacle opposite the entrance portico. Externally the dome is buttressed by volutes and the projecting porch is raised on steps, supported by columns and framed by giant pilasters under a gable. Only the Baroque coat of arms interrupts the Palladian geometry of the portico which corresponds with the recessed altar inside.

240   S. Andrea luxuriates in grey and white and reddish brown marble under the golden canopy of the dome. As the hexagonal coffers diminish in size towards the lantern, so the ribs broaden as they reach the cornice, where angels hold garlands suspended. Above the horizontal beams of the windows nude youths recline in the manner of Michelangelo's Ignudi. Nor is this surprising, for Bernini was essentially a sculptor. With all his Baroque love of curves and rhythmical movement, he remained a classicist in the proper use of architectural members, the giant pilasters and Corinthian columns supporting entablatures and pediments on massive plinths, the solidity and compactness of his structures where uprights and horizontals are in balance. Even the central plan of S. Andrea is in the Renaissance tradition and the elliptic interior is reflected in the multiple curves of the façade, from the great hemicycle of window and portico down to the ever widening semicircles of the gently graded steps. S. Andrea presents a perfect fusion of modified classical architecture with Baroque irruptions, especially in the decorative splendour of mottled marble, the figurative sculpture, the effects of light and of colour and the disciplined interplay of upright and curvilinear forms.

241   The Piazza S. Pietro which Bernini designed from 1656 onwards has a function similar to that of the enclosed atrium in the Early Christian basilica. But his sense for the grandiose translated this cloistered space into the dramatic vastness of an oval colonnade, open at the end, with an obelisk in the centre flanked by fountains and a narrower straight section channelling the faithful towards the church entrance. This breath-taking approach was preceded by narrow streets leading from the Ponte S. Angelo towards the widening piazza. But now a broad avenue, the Via della Conciliazione, has eliminated the element of surprise. By creating a 'corridor' in front of S. Peter's, as a prelude to the

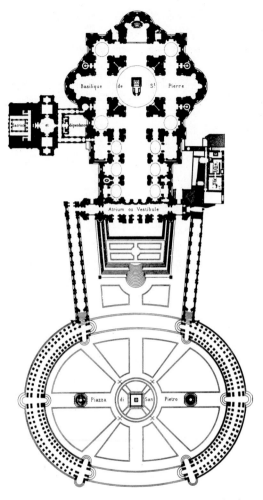

241. ROME. *Plan of S. Peter's and of the Bernini Colonnade (from Letarouilly)*

grand sweep of the colonnade and its movement of a universal embrace—a mighty gathering of Doric columns, four deep and carrying a straight **242** entablature—and by building the colonnade sufficiently low, Bernini counteracted the disproportion of the façade and also restored the full view of drum and dome. The far end of the oval is kept open, though originally Bernini intended closing it, so that an easy access is assured to the greatest number of pilgrims, as well as an unimpaired view.

242. ROME. *S. Peter's Square. Colonnade (photo: E.N.I.T. Rome)*

Moreover, at the northern end of the façade, as if to continue the colonnade into the palace, he created the Scala Regia, or ceremonial entrance—a tunnel-vaulted staircase under a triumphal arch, ornamented with the papal arms between two symbolic figures of fame. Perhaps no other church in Christendom has approaches of comparable dynamic and spectacular grandeur, not only on account of the shapely space enclosure, the dignified setting for the majestic building, a vast circumscribed arena for the Romans and all mankind to receive the pope's blessing, but also through the sculptural power and presence of these columns on their square bases, combining, under the sweeping entablature, into a unified whole.

Among other architectural projects of Bernini were the redesigning of the Louvre (1664-66) which did not come to fruition and the two Roman palaces Montecitorio and Chigi-Odescalchi.

The truism that Michelangelo remained a sculptor even in his great mural paintings applies *mutatis mutandis* also to Bernini whose architecture is statuesque, or else pictorial as in the Baldacchino and *Cattedra Petri* with its twisted columns, it clouds, rays, gyrating angels and ecstatic church fathers, creating a new Baroque genre comparable to the mystic levitation of saints. In his small churches Bernini was heir to the Renaissance, and he was close to Antiquity in his colonnade. The sculptural impulse is ever present in the spiritual themes, be it S. Andrew ascending or the ' statuesque ' columns in S. Peter's square. These columns

243. ROME. *S. Carlo alle Quattro Fontane. Oval Ceiling (photo: Gabinetto Fotografico Nazionale, Rome)*

converging upon the church and opening out to receive the faithful, echo in their elliptic shape Michelangelo's cupola above them. Finally the Scala Regia, a *trompe-l'oeil* with columns of diminishing height and narrowing flights of stairs feign by sculptural and pictorial means, in a limited space, a triumphal entrance to the Palace of the Pope.

By the side of Bernini's architecture the work of his sometime assistant, and later rival, Francesco Borromini (1599-1667) appears revolutionary and anti-classical. He was the true representative of the Roman full Baroque, whereas Bernini was bound by the forms of Graeco-Roman antiquity. Borromini had come to Rome in 1614 and for twenty years he had worked as an ornamental stone carver and architectural assistant to Maderno. After the latter's death he continued for a short while under Bernini until in 1633 he emerged fully fledged as an architect of genius, technically superior to his master as well as in the daring sophistication of his spatial geometry. To the theorists of classicism his work appeared extravagant, eccentric, even insane.

His first Roman enterprise was the small monastic church of the Trinitarians, S. Carlo alle Quattro Fontane, completed in 1641, one of the most exquisite space-creations in seventeenth-century Rome. Compared with its intricate but fully controlled plan and perimeter, its ever-changing

243

269

244. ROME. *S. Carlo alle Quattro Fontane. Part of façade (photo: E.N.I.T. Rome)*

244
245   contrasts of projecting and retreating wall surfaces, the extraordinary
246   web of cells composing the elliptic dome, S. Andrea al Quirinale seems
staid and static.

Borromoni's interior space is scanned by eight columns linking four major arches in the longitudinal and transversal directions. Concave bays and niches modify the ovoid plan of the church and fully rounded columns carry a heavy entablature all round the perimeter wall. The space between the paired columns contains not only the larger altar chapels, but also recesses for sculpture. These and the concave sections of the entablature contribute to the wave-like movement which culminates in the deeper cavities of the coffered apses. The paired columns in the four corners act as piers for the pendentive zone with disks filling the space between the main arches. Arches and disks act as tangents to the elliptical

245. ROME. *S. Carlo alle Quattro Fontane.* *Part of façade* (*photo: E.N.I.T. Rome*)

ring of the cupola which they support. This cupola is composed of polygonal cells and crosses—the crosses of the Trinitarians—diminishing in perspective recession towards the lantern and bounded by a strong frame of string courses and stylised foliage. The unified interior of S. Carlo builds up in three zones—iconological reference to the mystery of the Trinity, ' Tre et uno assieme ', as the inscription has it (three and one together)—columns, arches and dome, three groups of chapels, a theological conceit expressed in complex architectural terms.

The miracle of Borromini's first Roman masterpiece is its sense of movement, its shapeliness and illusionism, concealing its small scale. Its circumference is equal to one of the giant piers in S. Peter's. From the western entrance San Carlino unfolds its mystery in the diffused light from the coffered cupola—pentagonal grooves interspersed with crosses. The perfect oval of this half-dome cupola is held together by an ornamental

271

246. ROME. *S. Carlo alle Quattro Fontane. Cloisters (photo: E.N.I.T. Rome)*

band and the four tangent arches. Sixteen solid columns bear a continuous entablature and an empty frieze. The oval perimeter is varied by concave recesses of different size. Concurrently the columns spread out fast towards the widest part of the nave, contracting again at the sanctuary, to which the visitor is drawn compulsively. Shell niches with flame-like spikes and the writhing acanthus capitals enhance the movement, and

247. ROME. *S. Ivo della Sapienza (from G.B. Falda)*

even the abaci of the capitals are curved. Lastly, the four wider con-
cavities of the nave transform the lengthened ellipse into a Greek-cross
church.

Borromini's second Roman masterpiece which had its following
in Guarini's S. Sindone at Turin was the University church of S. Ivo
della Sapienza, started in 1648. At the far end of a large arcaded courtyard
by Giacomo della Porta a concave façade in two tiers and an attic with
four starry disks is the base of a great hexagonal drum whose convex
sections are separated by pilasters, thus counteracting the recessed
hemicycle of the façade. The ascending roof of S. Ivo is strengthened
by curved buttresses in line with the pilasters and crowned by an exotic
stepped spire whose concave sides are separated by twin columns. This
extraordinary shell encloses a space which is based on a hexagon within
a circle and divided into three large semicircular recesses opposite three
smaller convex bays and linked by huge rectangular piers. This elaborate
spatial design is echoed in the structure of the cupola whose ribs depart
from the corners of the piers in a wide sweeping movement without
intervening arches or pendentives towards the circular lantern. At the
widening base of the dome are large windows and above them papal
emblems and cherub heads.

S. Ivo is even more boldly conceived than S. Carlo, in its steep upward
surge, the continuity of piers and ribs and the echoing of the ground
plan radiation in the starry cupola. Externally the corresponding concavi-
ties of façade and drum are resolved first in the curved roof-buttresses

248. ROME. *Oratory of S. Filippo Neri*

then in the elegant lantern, the oriental spire and the iron ball and cross at the summit, precariously balanced on a fanciful wrought-iron structure. Though della Porta's courtyard and exedra-like façade of S. Ivo were already in being when Borromini undertook to build the church, he yet created an organic whole by inventing the complementary shape of the drum with its convex sections and the graceful superstructure of the lantern. Here the volutes lead up to a tempietto, and hence to the torch-like pinnacles and flaming crown which, on its airy metal frame,

249. ROME. *S. Agnese in Piazza Navona*

sends up into the Roman sky the symbols of Christian dominion, the cross surmounting the globe.

For the Jubilee year of 1650 Borromini restored the interior of S. Giovanni in Laterano by enclosing the nave pillars in square piers, faced by a giant order of pilasters with tabernacle niches containing statues of the apostles. The Early Christian basilica which had been threatened with ruin underwent a resplendent Baroque transformation.

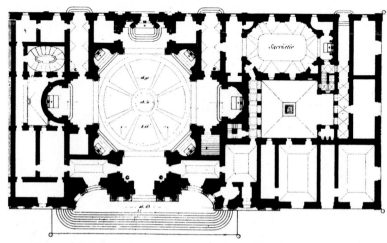

250. ROME. *S. Agnese (and College) in Piazza Navona (from Letarouilly)*

Retaining its wood ceiling, the nave presents an even rhythm of lofty piers alternating with lower arches and enhanced by aedicules, relief panels and other wall ornaments.

Coeval with the elaborate and unorthodox S. Carlo alle Quattro **248** Fontane is Borromini's Oratory of S. Filippo Neri or at least the façade for the building of the monastery extended over a decade. The Oratory stands next to the church of the Filippines, the Chiesa Nuova, and in spite of its apparent symmetry demonstrates the principal trends of Baroque architecture, mass and movement, swelling and retreating forms. In the façade verticalism is stressed by the two orders of pilasters framing the five bays of the central block, though the projecting cornices emphasize the horizontal. But the main feature is the inward curve of the façade and the contrast between the two central bays in the upper and lower storey, convex and concave respectively. Moreover, the great crowning pediment is composed of two curves and a triangle, forms which recur in the rounded or angular cornices over the windows. The ornamental detail of the façade consists of variations of these basic shapes, with the richest decoration in the central bays. The Oratory blends unity and compactness with diversity of detail. Like the later Collegio di Propaganda Fide the street frontage of the Oratory is as much a house or palace as an ecclesiastical building.

249 The façade of S. Agnese in Piazza Navona (1653-57) alongside the **250** famous square is Borromini's response to the church of S. Peter's. Inside, he replaced the Greek-cross plan of Rainaldi by an elliptical central space inscribed within a regular octagon which is stressed by the entablature projecting above the corner pillars, and by lengthening the arms of the crossing. But the chief glory of S. Agnese is its lucid façade and elegant dome, flanked by perforated twin towers. Borromini had to design a church front in line with the neighbouring palaces to be taken in at a glance from the opposite side. He made the façade and balusters curve inward with the central features of portico, drum and dome recessed and rising in a continuous sequence of columns, pilasters and ribs. The sections of the high drum are set back in space and the graceful shape of dome and lantern, the classical portico between paired columns and the flanking towers are a fulfilment of what the façade of S. Peter's might have been. The beautifully proportioned whole, including the dome, is in full view of the beholder.

The encased cupola and campanile of S. Andrea della Fratte, begun in 1653, are among the most extravagant creations of Borromini, enhanced by their contrasting shapes. For the dome is really a shallow-roofed drum with diagonally projecting columnar ends. Concave sections frame a convex bay in the centre with a large window between giant columns so that the now familiar undulating rhythm of wall surfaces results.

This weighty drum-like structure serves as a foil for the detached bell-tower rising in three tiers of contrasting and ever more fragile sections. On a solid base which repeats the diagonal columnar projections of the drum, rises a miniature temple with open colonnade, multiple rings and balusters; on its roof top angel herms, their wings lowered, act as caryatids for the delicate superstructure of sinuous shapes, scrolls, volutes and pinnacles and on the summit a spiky crown. This imaginative belfry is the most anti-classical of Baroque inventions, though antique elements are used like the round temple, herms and columns.

Borromini's contribution to the architecture of the Roman Baroque was ' to mould space and mass ' according to precise geometrical concepts and ornamental motifs. The genius for handling mass, movement and spatial illusionism, as in the gallery of Palazzo Spada, he shared with other media of Baroque art. As an inventor of taut and sinuous sculptural shapes in an architectural context he was unrivalled. It is customary to compare the work and character of the two protagonists of the Roman Baroque; Borromini a solitary, unstable and melancholy artist, contemptuous of wealth and of fame who, in a fit of madness died by his own sword, and Bernini, fortune's favourite whose brilliant career is a sequence of triumphs.

Both artists present the high summer of the Baroque. Yet in architecture Borromini was the revolutionary. Though he worked on a smaller, more intimate scale and created nothing comparable to the antique grandeur of the colonnade of S. Peter's—his rejection of classical calm and

277

T

regularity and his novel use of undulating walls and crescent façades, of delicately wrought belfries and cupolas—worlds apart from Bernini's solid hemicycle at Ariccia—are a complete break with Renaissance tradition. Borromini's style differed from the scenic character and panache of his great rival by his precision of ornamental detail, the curvilinear rhythm of tympana, of volutes supporting urns or spires, of sinuous shapes suggestive of movement. In the whole field of Baroque architecture Borromini's work which his detractors judged 'corrupt' and 'chimerical' was the most ingenious, shapely, lucid and coherent.

The disciplined and complex geometry of Borromini's designs and ground plans is based on the interplay of oval, circle and triangle. The interior of S. Carlo is oval, but that of S. Ivo is a hexagon contained by a circle. The basic module of both plans is the double triangle erected over the central axis. The interior of S. Agnese—Rainaldi's design modified by Borromini—forms a regular octagon surrounding a circle. The octagonal structure is emphasized by projecting cornices. Strange fact that the most dynamic architect of the Roman full Baroque organized space according to subtle geometrical schemes. Their complementary shapes are as exhilarating in the preliminary drawings as in the finished edifices.

The third of the great creative artists of seventeenth century Rome, Pietro da Cortona (1596-1669) was first and foremost a mural painter. The ceiling in the *Gran Salone* of Palazzo Barberini and the decorations in the Pitti are his principal claim to fame. Yet like Bernini with whom he shared the undisputed leadership of the Baroque movement at its peak, he was active in more than one field, painting easel pictures and advising Pope Urban VIII on architectural projects.

251 Cortona built the first full-powered Baroque church in Rome: SS. Martina e Luca, begun in 1635. Based on a Greek-cross plan with a weighty cupola over the crossing, it is the most sculptural of all Baroque churches in Rome, though, in contrast to Bernini, entirely devoid of figurative sculpture. All round the walls and apsidal ends are columns, pilasters, niches; and the vaults and dome are overlaid with rich ornamental reliefs. The plastic effects of the interior are obtained by recessive movements of architectural members. Pilasters at the four arms of the crossing alternate with Ionian columns, softly rounded with sharply angular forms under a zigzagging cornice. Vaults and cupola have moulded ornaments and their ribs stand out from the coffers, rosettes and festoons. The church is radiantly white and its powerful impact based on a succession of planar and sculptural forms breaks up the wall surfaces into three zones of graded recession or projection. The exterior of SS. Martina e Luca is designed in two orders over a convex plan;

251. ROME. *SS. Martina e Luca*

the columns below are embedded in the façade and continued in the members, framing door and tabernacle-window respectively. The façade repeats the advancing and retreating planes of the interior.

The two subsequent churches by Pietro da Cortona are progressively Roman, just as in his paintings he employs classical motifs like the round temple in the *Sacrifice to Diana*. His most original work is the façade and piazza of S. Maria della Pace of 1656-57. A slightly convex upper storey, crowned by a segmental pediment within a triangular one, is raised over a semi-circular colonnaded portico. This projecting peristyle,

252,
253
(187)

279

252. Rome. *S. Maria della Pace*

carried on Doric columns, links the church to the piazza, while the whole edifice is embraced at the back by concave wings. By contrast the façade of S. Maria in via Lata (1662) abandons the concave-convex relationship between the storeys, evolved by Borromini, for a severely Roman structure of free-standing columns in the portico, supporting a straight entablature, and a triumphal arch motif in the loggia above.

Cortona's architecture which he himself regarded only as of secondary importance, appears at first sight irreconcilable with his painterly style, the handling of great masses in movement, the riotous colour and amorphous background of clouds. But in SS. Martina e Luca he enlarges the scope of Baroque construction in a kindred way, dissolving static walls into constantly varying planes by moving giant columns in and out with plastic intent rather than to define spatial units like bays or chapels. In S. Maria della Pace he applied Borromini's inward and outward pressing

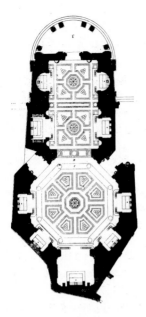

253. ROME. *S. Maria della*
Pace (from Letarouilly)

curvilinear walls in a highly original form, creating a grand proscenium
as background to a piazza; only in his last building did he abandon Baroque
dynamics and flexibility for the revived grandeur of Imperial Rome.

Apart from Bernini, Borromini and Cortona, the prodigious church
building and town planning programme of the Roman full Baroque was
carried out by Martino Longhi the Younger (1602-60) and Carlo Rainaldi
(1611-91). The church of SS. Vincenzo ed Anastasio was completed in
1650 by Martino Longhi. Borromini's alternating rhythm of concave-
convex wall surfaces and Longhi's two-tier portico with straight walling and
groups of triple columns framing the centre, reveal contrasting principles
of Baroque church façades. It has a broad lower storey with classical
entablature and two segmental pediments over the entrance, and a lofty
superstructure of about half its width, rising freely like a temple and
tenuously linked to its base by two slender volutes. The upper tier is
crowned by a triangular pediment over a broken segment, and fragments
of the entablature move forward, close to the sculptured angels supporting
a large coat of arms above the window recess. The free standing columns
of the upper storey are held in firm embrace by the gable, and this enhances
its unity, whereas the lower storey extends to the corner columns by
means of blank wall areas. The rich articulation and massiveness of

architectural members and the fanciful, even Mannerist variations on classical themes contribute to one of the most powerful and shapely church façades of the Roman Baroque.

The style of Carlo Rainaldi was equally monumental and scenographic. At S. Maria in Campitelli he used fully rounded columns on mighty plinths, framing recessed aedicula in both storeys, each crowned by a broken pediment and a zigzagging fragmentation of cornices. Rainaldi was also a town planner and designed the twin churches in Piazza del Popolo which face the traveller entering Rome from the north by the Porta del Popolo. These near identical churches, S. Maria di Monte Santo and S. Maria de' Miracoli are the terminal points of the great square from which three straight avenues radiate into the city centre. Their domes and airy bell-towers and temple-like porticoes, with free-standing columns supporting a broad entablature and triangular pediment, proclaim the classical tendencies of the Late Baroque. This severe classicism of the porticoes is due to Bernini's intervention in Rainaldi's work during the 1670s.

In Venice the architecture of the full Baroque culminates in one man and in one building, the imposing dome and marble clad octagon with volutes of S. Maria della Salute by Baldassare Longhena, dominating the entrance to the Grand Canal. It is for the skyline of Venice what S. Peter's is for Rome. The image of the monumental 'Rotunda' has been proliferated and romanticised by the impressionist brush of Francesco Guardi. There, in the changing lights and reflecting water of the lagoon the Salute assumes the character of a mirage. But the reality of its structure has more substance, it is in fact one of the most powerful and thought-out creations of the Italian Baroque. Longhena was born in the same year as Bernini and his immensely active life spans the same period (1598-1680). The Salute, his youthful masterpiece, was built as a votive church for the Virgin after the plague of 1630. Longhena won the competition by his design of a centrally planned church, favoured by Renaissance architects, against the more conventional Latin-cross plan of his rivals.

Longhena, Scamozzi's pupil, was trained as a sculptor and architect. He created many funerary monuments for Venetian churches and in the Salute the figures rising on columns and volutes and the large dome itself with its cover of lead, the high octagonal drum and the huge spiral scroll-buttresses, linking drum and projecting chapels, are powerful plastic shapes. Each of the six chapels has a classicising façade, complete with a small order of columns and pilasters, segmental windows and gable, whereas the main entrance to the church leads through a triumphal arch, flanked by giant columns on high pedestals.

254

254. VENICE. *S. Maria della Salute*

This severely structural exterior, modified only by the fanciful
scrolls and eloquent sculptures—with a simpler subsidiary dome over
the sanctuary between two campanili—is the prelude to an equally lucid
interior. The model of an octagonal, centrally planned church with
ambulatory and apses flanking the presbytery can be found in S. Vitale,
Ravenna. But Longhena's interior is different through the introduction
of chapels beyond the arcading of the central octagon. These are inter-
connected by the circular passage or ambulatory and used with great
scenic effect; for the deep recesses of the six altar chapels radiate from the
centre. The corners of the octagon are stressed by applied columns,

283

255. VENICE. *Palazzo Pesaro (photo: Italian Institute, London)*

each on a high podium and continued upwards into the drum by statues
and pilasters, flanking round-headed windows. The greatest effect
of longitudinal progress is obtained by the view from the entrance through
a succession of arches towards the High Altar, terminated by the triple-
arched wall of the choir. The structure of the interior is marked colour-
istically by the grey of columns and architectural members against the
white-washed walls. A kind of balcony surrounds the base of the drum.
This and the statues, cornice and Corinthian capitals are the only mellow-
ing elements in the austerity of the interior. The Salute differs from the
dynamics of the Roman full Baroque by the lucidity of its spatial logic.

In civic architecture Longhena's greatest achievements were the
Palazzi Rezzonico and Pesaro. They depend from Jacopo Sansovino's
255 Palazzo Corner and Libreria Vecchia of the previous century. Palazzo
Pesaro is grander and more ornately Baroque than Jacopo's High Renaissance building, with deeply recessed windows between columns on high
bases and a sculptural frieze beneath the cornice. In place of the third

256. ROME. *The Spanish Steps, and Trinità dei Monti* (photo: E.N.I.T. Rome)

257. ROME. *The Treves Fountain* (*photo: E.N.I.T. Rome*)

258. ROME. *S. Giovanni in Laterano with Galilei's façade*

portal a niche-fountain has been placed in the centre of the ground
floor. Sansovino's restraint and repose have been modified by the potent
plasticity of rusticated blocks and a profusion of sculptural ornament.
Cupids fill the pendentives of window arches and giant figures the openings
between paired columns. A continuous balcony runs the whole width
of the *piano nobile*. The character of Longhena's palace is conditioned
by the luminous stresses upon sculptural forms, the multiple columns
of the upper storeys, the diamond-shaped cyclopic blocks of the basement,
on keystones and carved heads in contrast to the dark cavities of portals
and windows, resulting in a baroque ' dissolution ' of wall surfaces.

Some of the famous sights of Rome belong to the later stages of the
Baroque and the birth of the Rococo. The Spanish steps by Francesco de   256
Sanctis (1723-25) winding their way in a broad sinuous flight in and out
of terraces and ramps to the Trinità dei Monti, were designed for the near
as well as the distant view and is equally effective from the long and narrow
approaches of the lane as from the wide Piazza di Spagna at its foot.
Its spacious and gentle ascent at the end of an interminable tunnel of
houses has all the graces of the eighteenth century.

Among other urbanistic highlights of Rome are the Piazza S.
Ignazio and Fontana Trevi. The latter, designed by Nicola Salvi has   257
the background of a palace façade with a great niche or exedra in the
centre, containing the statue of bearded Neptune in a flowing cloak.
This high-powered baroque application of classical architecture is the
foil to a Rococo tumble of marine gods and sea horses among Rococo
shells and natural rocks and spraying water, reminiscent of Bernini's
Fountain of the Four Rivers. It is a scenic spectacle which enlivens the

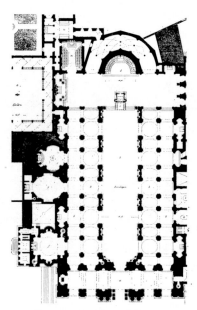

259. ROME. *S. Giovanni in Laterano*
(*from Letarouilly*)

sweeping round of a basin upon which the visitor comes unawares from narrow lanes. Equally designed for the near view and endowed with the same element of suddenness and surprise is Piazza S. Ignazio by Raguzzini, and here it is not the broad façade of the church but the small shapely palaces confining the square with their straight wings and crescent fronts which make its intimate and aristocratic appeal.

258
259   Galilei's façade of the Lateran basilica, though built at the height of the Rococo (1737), is remarkable for its staid classical character, harmonious proportions and vertical stresses, especially in the giant order of paired columns framing the central entrance and loggia under a gabled tympanum. It recalls Maderno's portico of S. Peter's. The rigorous symmetry of the façade is based on the correspondence between the five doorways leading into the narthex and the five tall arches of the upper loggia and on the even rhythm of giant pilasters separating the dark openings with strong chiaroscuro effects beneath the widely projecting cornice. As twin columns frame the centre so the end walls are strengthened by paired pilasters and the whole square edifice testifies to an uncompromisingly classical trend devoid of curvilinear forms. Only the swaying statues of mitred popes on top of the roof balusters and the crowning centre piece with the risen Christ introduce a period element of the eighteenth century Rococo.

260. ROME. *Basilica of S. Maria Maggiore*

Less stringently modelled on the Antique is Ferdinando Fuga's slightly later façade of S. Maria Maggiore (1743). But though the scale and relationship of the two storeys are similar—as is the emphasis on the main entrance and Benediction Loggia—the overall impression is more elegant and gracious. The façade is in line with two flanking palaces of equal height and its upper section of three lofty arches is harmoniously linked with the five openings below. Triangular and segmental tympana with figure sculpture and a Madonna and Child silhouetted against the sky animate the resplendent façade which uses the architectural elements of S. Giovanni in Laterano to richer and more pictorial effects.

In southern Italy the greatest architectural enterprise of the eighteenth century is the Royal Palace of Caserta, commissioned in 1752 by the Bourbon king Charles III from an Italianized Dutch architect van Wittel or Vanvitelli (1700-73). The very scale and nature of the building vied with Versailles and other international courtly residences. It is 600 feet long and the central feature is a pedimented temple front which breaks

260
(5, 6)

261

261. CASERTA. *Royal Palace (photo: E.P.T. Caserta)*

262. CASERTA. *Royal Palace. Grand staircase (photo: E.P.T. Caserta)*

the monotony of an otherwise austere and interminable block with projecting ends. The high ground floor is built of oblong rusticated stones and the only articulation is the colossal order in the centre and at the sides where towers were planned. The lay-out of the palace is almost square with intersecting wings, dividing the huge space into four inner courts. There are octagonal vestibules on both levels with surprise vistas in many directions through courtyards and formal gardens. The vestibules with surrounding passages were inspired by Longhena's central octagon and ambulatory in the Salute. A magnificent ceremonial staircase leads to a landing, then splits into two flights along the walls **262** to reach the upper vestibule with its three arches and coffered vault. The Palace of Caserta is classicist rather than Rococo; and in spite of the inexorable logic inherent in its regular plan is animated by surprise effects due to Vanvitelli's skill and experience as a designer of stage sets.

Besides Rome, it is Piedmont and its capital Turin which, between 1650 and 1750, developed the style of the late Baroque in a series of magnificent buildings. Turin is also the most modern and systematically planned city, designed as a residence for the dukes of Savoy. Two architects of genius, Guarino Guarini (1624-83) and Filippo Juvarra (1678-1736) determined its seventeenth and eighteenth century aspect.

Guarini, poet, mathematician and philosopher who also wrote a treatise *Architettura Civile*, was born in Modena and worked in places as far apart as Messina and Lisbon, Paris and Rome. In 1639 he entered

265. TURIN. *Cupola of S. Lorenzo*

265   The complexities of S. Lorenzo are even more subtle, the interplay of spatial units still richer and more varied. Upon an octagonal exterior with concave sides and large oval windows rises a high drum on twin columns, supporting a small dome. Internally the eight walls of the octagon are leaping forward convex fashion, but are broken up by deeply recessed altar chapels flanked by white statues in niches. Wide open arches on red marble columns form a festive entrance to these recessed spaces. A continuous curvilinear cornice is the base of the drum and here broad arches span triforium galleries, and intervening pendentives support the cupola. Thus inside and out there are three consecutive zones, octagon, drum and dome. But the strangest geometry is found in 266 the interior rib-scaffolding of the cupola, made transparent by the light from the lantern and oculi windows. These segmental ribs are overlapping and interlaced, a mere skeleton, supporting nothing. They make a geometrical pattern, dissolving the solidity of the walls in a manner comparable to the Gothic. Their intersections coalesce into ' an eight-cornered star of ribs '. By their mysterious effects of light filtering through the fragile web, Guarini's cupolas establish a link with the supernatural. They are the expression of late Baroque sophistication

294

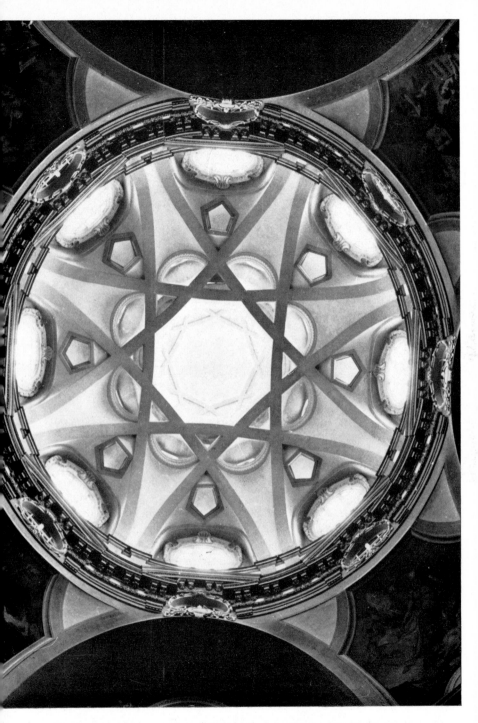

266. TURIN. *S. Lorenzo. Inside of cupola (photo: E.P.T. Turin)*

267. TURIN. *Palazzo Madama* (*photo: E.P.T. Turin*)

as is the intermingling of interior spaces, their ceaseless forward and inward movement, linking one convex area to another at sharp angles within the circumference of circle or octagon.

Almost a generation separates Filippo Juvarra from Guarino Guarini and his style is distinguished by simple grandeur rather than sophistication. Born in Messina, Juvarra spent ten years in Rome in the studio of Carlo Fontana, absorbing the architectural legacy of Antiquity and Renaissance and also the more recent ventures of Bernini and Borromini. Son of a silversmith, a keen draughtsman and stage designer, Juvarra was a mature architect when in 1714 Vittorio Amadeo II summoned him to the court of Turin. There he began an immense activity and during the remaining twenty-two years of his life he built five churches and four royal palaces in and around Turin and also contributed to the urban planning of the city. His finest achievements are Palazzo Madama, the Royal Hunting Lodge of Stupinigi and the Basilica of La Superga. Palazzo Madama (1718-21) is really a resplendent façade screening a medieval castle. The richly defined frontage with its rusticated basement and magnificent first floor whose fluted columns mark out the projecting centre from the pilaster divisions of the wings, its nine round-headed

268. TURIN. *Palazzo Madama. Grand staircase* (*photo: E.P.T. Turin*)

windows of large size, its balconies and balusters, roof sculptures and
stucco decorations conceals one of the grandest and most luminous staircases of the Baroque extending along the whole width of the façade.
This staircase is one of the most magnificent of the Baroque, a lofty **268**

end of the Basilica where the separate altar room is, like the portico, an extension of the central space, the church is joined to the monastery, concealing part of its brick façade. In the regularity of geometrical bodies, the application of classical orders, the organic unity of the whole, and not least by its elevated position the Superga combines Neo-classical features with the Renaissance ideal of the rounded and domed temple. Internally four arches and a circular entablature, fluted columns enclosing niches, and a lofty drum without pendentives under the ribbed dome, compose a sumptuous and elegant interior in the eighteenth century style, lightly painted in yellow and blue. To the restless interlocking spaces of Guarini, Juvarra opposes his regular design, calm and serene and monumental, a triumph of logical space-construction in the age of enlightenment.

CONCLUSION

On the Growth and Planning of the Italian Cities

A historical survey and analysis of Italian architecture should perhaps be concluded by a quick glance at town planning, the growth of cities and their characteristic sites, lest in the preoccupation with styles, individual architects and monuments the overall picture of Italian cities be lost. For a city is more than the sum total of its famous buildings, scattered across plain or hillside; it is the product of history, of natural growth and topography, conditioned by social and economic causes, the need for shelter and defence, but also willed by man and his aesthetic propensities.

Few cities can boast undisturbed logical planning; most of them grew piece-meal through the ages and were fortunate if their most beautiful sights were not obliterated by mean or tasteless dwellings. In the Middle-Ages houses clustered around the protective strongholds of their overlords; but pride of place belonged to the ecclesiastical buildings, the triad of cathedral, bell-tower and baptistery. Giotto's tower beside the Duomo and octagonal baptistery in Florence or the incomparable lay-out of the Campo dei Miracoli at Pisa: Leaning Tower, Cathedral, Rotunda and Camposanto, or the smaller compound in Romanesque Parma come to mind.

Thinking of Florence or Venice, of Padua or Rome, we visualise its domes first of all; then its civic buildings and wide open squares. Frequently these lead up to a resplendent church façade like the piazza S. Croce in Florence, the vast square in front of the Frari at Venice or to the seat of government, the Palazzo Pubblico in Siena enclosed by the amphitheatre of its Campo. In medieval days, and even in the Renaissance they served for tournaments as well as for the gathering of the people or as open markets. Few Italian towns are without their Piazza delle Erbe, and often, as in Padua, the principal building is the Court of Justice: Palazzo della Ragione, heir to the pagan basilica of the Romans.

A theoretical basis for town planning came in with the Renaissance treatises on architecture, based on Vitruvius like Alberti's *De Re Aedificatoria* or Filarete's *Trattato di Architettura*. But the first realisation of an ideal city was created by Pope Pius II, unique expression of the humanist desire for fame and the classical unity of style engendered by the early Renaissance architects and theorists. Bernardo Rossellino, Alberti's pupil, built the Cathedral at Pienza birthplace of Pope Pius, and two flanking palaces around a square which were like the walls

273

273. VENICE. *Aerial view of S. Mark's Square*

encompassing an interior space and leading towards the broad cathedral front, not in parallel but in ' diverging ' lines. The city square of Pienza, built around 1460 was an enclosed, inward looking space.

By contrast Ferrara, under its enlightened ruler Ercole d'Este and his architect Biagio Rossetti, was enlarged around 1492 beyond its medieval limits, its space doubled and its regular network of streets continued and linked with the surrounding country. Great oblong palaces like Palazzo Diamanti stressed the straightness and perspective of these streets.

Renaissance Florence does not seem to have followed a concerted plan. The Florentines were an individualistic race and here we look for single monuments of personal stamp and character rather than unified planning. Her modern image was formed during the fifteenth century by a succession of great architects like Alberti, Brunelleschi, Michelozzo and their followers. The basilican churches of S. Lorenzo and S. Spirito with their Roman colonnades, the graceful loggias of the Innocenti, Alberti's façade of S. Maria Novella, giving focus to the square and his Palazzo Rucellai employing the three classical orders, were the first truly Renaissance buildings in Florence. In the Medici and Strozzi palaces impenetrable strength of the outer walls was joined to the grace of the inner courts. Only in the sixteenth century did an area of urban planning come to Florence in the shape of Vasari's Uffizi, two long palace-wings with decorative detail derived from Michelangelo, linking Palazzo Vecchio

274. ROME. *Piazza del Campidoglio. Palazzo Senatorio*

with the river Arno, a long and narrow corridor of a street bridged by an archway on the riverside.

No unified plan can be claimed for the city of Rome, though successive popes and architects of the sixteenth and seventeenth centuries left their mark upon the spiritual centre of the catholic world and the graveyard of Antiquity. Under Julius II and Leo X Bramante and Raphael surveyed and measured classical ruins as Brunelleschi and Donatello had done before them, and in their domed churches and noble palaces, they and their followers Peruzzi and Sangallo continued and modified the classical tradition. The greatest impact upon the urban landscape of Rome was made by Michelangelo's massive dome of S. Peter and, in secular architecture, his Piazza del Campidoglio. As Florence was dominated architecturally by Brunelleschi's cupola and topographically by the river Arno, so was Rome by the river Tiber and Michelangelo's dome. S. Peter's suffered later modifications in shape and plan, extending towards the city by Maderno's nave and even more by Bernini's all-embracing colonnade. On the Capitol hill Michelangelo was given the task in 1537 of reconstructing its buildings and lay-out, a grand task of town planning such as Bernardo Rossellino had accomplished on an intimate scale for Pope Pius II in his city of Pienza, designing a cathedral flanked by palaces. In the Piazza del Campidoglio, Michelangelo created a civic compound worthy of the Roman past, a volume of space enclosed on three sides by well defined palace façades. He emphasized the axial viewpoint, leading from the flight of steps at the entrance towards the campanile and staircase of the Senators' palace. He gave the piazza an inward looking shape and confined the two façades

274
275

305

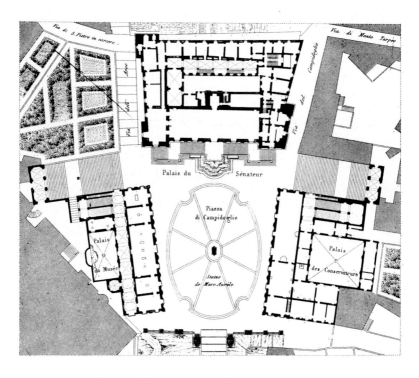

275. ROME. *Piazza del Campidoglio (from Letarouilly)*

of the flanking palaces to two storeys with open porticoes and a giant order of pilasters. The large, square openings are not arches, but have a straight entablature supported by columns. Columns recur in the tabernacle windows. Verticals and horizontals are evenly balanced and continued all round the square. The three palaces are crowned by balusters. The shape of the piazza was enhanced by the oval design of the paving and stressed by placing in its centre the equestrian statue of Marcus Aurelius.

The Piazza del Campidoglio presents a unique example of town planning, a grand climax of the Capitoline Hill to be taken in at one glance. The two side palaces converge towards the triangular ramp of the Senators' stairway. Michelangelo's disciplined co-ordination of individual architectural shapes, like the segmental and triangular pediments of the windows between the pilasters, raised on high sockets, are subordinated to the dramatic impact of the whole piazza which has been aptly described as ' an outdoor room with three walls '.

Later popes, and especially Pius IV (1559-65) and Sixtus V (1585-90) made greater strides towards the systematization of Rome. Straight avenues were devised like Via Pia, terminated by Michelangelo's Porta Pia, as well as the Corso—Rome's greatest thoroughfare. Under Sixtus V S. Maria Maggiore his favourite basilica became the centre of a starlike radiation of streets connecting the great pilgrimage churches of Rome with each other. His architect and city planner was Domenico Fontana (1543-1607) who rebuilt the huge pile of the Lateran Palace and imposed a network of long avenues confined between the unadorned and unending walls of palace façades. The first completed road was the Via Felice (1587) reaching in a long sweep to Trinità dei Monti. At the crossing with Via Pia were the four corner fountains which gave their name to Borromini's church of S. Carlo alle Quattro Fontane. He also created waterworks such as the Acqua Felice supplying the famous fountains of Rome. The time was ripe for the great Baroque transformation of the city which came in the wake of Bernini and Cortona, Borromini and Rainaldi.

Notwithstanding Fontana's master plan of axial avenues, the *Piano Regolatore*, piazzas with fountains or obelisks played an even larger role than thoroughfares. These were of two principal kinds, vast and designed for the view from afar, often towards a great church like S. Peter's and Il Gesù or the Piazza del Popolo which was the northern gateway to the Urbs, root and focal point of three famous streets issuing between twin churches towards the city centre; or else small and intimate courts such as Piazza S. Ignazio and S. Maria della Pace or the restricted surround of the Fontana Trevi. In the eighteenth century, perhaps under French influence, the long view towards some exhilarating Rococo sight was preferred, like de Sancti's sinuous Spanish Steps rising from Piazza Spagna to the Trinità dei Monti.

In Central Italy, Umbria and the Marches, fine city centres, lined by late medieval palaces were carved out of encroaching rocks and hills as in Todi or Gubbio, whereas Urbino can boast the finest palace of the Early Renaissance, rising sheer, above a deep gorge, with twin towers and triumphal arches; this is the Ducal Palace, a fortified castle and princely dwelling with many wings and courts generously laid out and exquisitely decorated.

Venice is like no other city in Italy and the world. Her ' Corso ' is a broad waterway, lined by munificent palaces and domed churches, her lanes and squares, her calli and campi unexpectedly give on to a church façade, her housefronts rise steeply from the black mirror of the lagoon and countless bridges span the network not of streets, but of canals. The incomparable Piazza S. Marco, a long trapezoid space, bounded by the porticoes of the Procuratie and leading towards the five-domed Basilica is like a gigantic open air state-room, designed for the seething life and the pageantries of the Republic.

The Piazzetta between Ducal Palace and Libreria Vecchia is its orthogonal extension towards the vast basin of the Molo, looking across to the islands of S. Giorgio Maggiore and the Giudecca. Here the churches of Palladio with their white classical porticoes, grey domes and pink walls melt into the distance of sky and water, but they also form a colouristic link with Palazzo Ducale and the Byzantine church of S. Mark's.

Palladio who transformed his native city of Vicenza in a distinctive classical style where Roman *gravitas* combined with Venetian light and colour, was perhaps the greatest urban architect of the second half of the sixteenth century. He built the palaces of the aristocracy along the main axis of the city and on both sides of the street. Such palaces were of modified Roman character; some severely classical, some Mannerist or even proto-Baroque. Their façades were designed for the perspective view and also to be seen from below. That accounts for their high plinths and giant orders—pilasters or engaged columns—and also for their decorations—carved reliefs, capitals, balusters—in the well-lit upper storeys. Palladio's villas and palaces in and around Vicenza as well as his Venetian churches were conceived in harmony with the urban or landscape setting. His rotundas and temple fronts, his orders and entablatures were a complete renascence of the Latin grammar of form. A secular basilica of monumental proportions became the city centre of Vicenza and the Loggia del Capitano facing it was a richly moulded triumphal arch of the Romans. In Palladio's Vicenza the ideal city of the fifteenth century humanists found its historical fulfilment where the Roman past was recreated in domestic architecture and inextricably linked with the life of a modern city.

Two other cities in the north of Italy are renowned for systematic planning: Genoa and Turin. At Genoa, during the second half of the sixteenth century, the nobility began to build palaces on the mountain slopes dominating the town. A new street, the Strada Nuova, was begun by Galeazzo Alessi in 1551 and continued by Rocco Lurago. The palaces located here had to be built on different levels and the problem was solved by unifying hall, courtyard and ceremonial staircase as an ascending whole. What Lurago achieved in Palazzo Doria, Bartolommeo Bianco developed in the magnificent Baroque University of 1606-18. The palaces of Genoa alongside newly created streets adhered to the hallowed tradition of having individual façades.

But the systematic transformation of Turin into a populous and capital city, begun by the Dukes of Savoy in the 1560s and continued for over two centuries of creative building activity was a larger enterprise, involving rapid growth and systematic planning and unified frontages. Chief architects under Carlo Emanuele I (1580-1630) were Vittozzi and Castellamonte. The Roman and medieval town was modernised and enlarged by a network of parallel streets and unified piazzas; most conspicuous the Via Roma and the Piazza S. Carlo (1638). Probably under French influence the traditional emphasis on characteristic palace façades was abandoned in favour of geometrical and regular lay-out of streets. The great square was enclosed by porticoes, and the city expanded towards the river Po. But during the seventeenth and eighteenth centuries, Turin became one of the great Baroque cities of Europe through the distinctive styles of two architects of genius—Guarini and Juvarra—who created in the capital of this northern province—Piedmont, an equivalent of Borromini's structural intricacies. The systematic enlargement of this great industrial centre and most modern of all Italian cities, came to fruition in the course of the twentieth century.

V

BIBLIOGRAPHY

SOURCE BOOKS

Vitruvius, *De architectura, Ten Books.* Roman. Early first century A.D. Principal architectural treatise of Antiquity from which all Renaissance theory depends. First printed edition, Rome 1486. Edited and illustrated by Fra Giocondo, Venice 1511

Alberti, Leon Battista, *De re aedificatoria.* Ten books, based on Vitruvius. Published posthumously, Florence 1485

Francesco di Giorgio, *Treatise on Architecture, c.* 1456 (*Trattato di architettura*)

Filarete, *Trattato di architettura, c.* 1464

Serlio, Sebastiano, *L'architettura.* Six books, 1537-51. Two books of architectural drawings published posthumously in 1575. Vast collection of classical motifs based on Bramante and Raphael. Practical sourcebook

Vignola, Giacomo, *Regola delli cinque ordini d'architettura,* 1562. Copper engravings of the five Orders

Palladio, Andrea, *I quattro libri dell'architettura.* Venice, 1570. The Orders, palaces and villas including Palladio's own civic buildings, temples

Scamozzi, Vincenzo, *Dell'idea dell'architettura universale,* Venice 1615. Depends from Palladio. Influenced the classical revival of the eighteenth century

OTHER BOOKS FOR FURTHER STUDY

Ackerman, James S., *The Architecture of Michelangelo,* 2 vols. Rev. ed. London 1966

—— *Palladio,* Harmondsworth 1966

Argan, Giuliano C., *The Renaissance City,* London/New York, 1969

Briggs, Martin S., *Everyman's Concise Encyclopaedia of Architecture,* London 1959

Bucci, Mario, *La basilica di Sta. Croce,* Firenze 1965

Carli, Enzo and Gian Alberto dell'Acqua, *Profilo dell'arte italiana,* 2 vols, Bergamo 1955

Chierici, Gino, *Il palazzo italiano,* Milano 1964

Conant, Kenneth John, *Carolingian and Romanesque Architecture 800-1200,* Harmondsworth 1959

Decker, H., *Romanesque Art in Italy,* London 1958

Fleming, J., H. Honour, N. Pevsner, *Penguin Dictionary of Architecture,* Harmondsworth 1967

Fletcher, Sir Banister, *A History of Architecture,* London 1961

Franklin, J. W., *The Cathedrals of Italy,* London 1958

Gnone, Tommaso, *Dizionario architettonico illustrato,* Torino 1967

Golzio, Vincenzo, *Seicento e settecento,* 2 vols, Torino 1960

Krautheimer, Richard, *Early Christian and Byzantine Architecture,* Harmondsworth 1965

Lees-Milne, James, *Roman Mornings,* London 1956

Letarouilly, Paul, *Edifices de Rome Moderne,* Paris 1868 (London 1944)

Letarouilly, Paul, *The Vatican,* ed. by Sir A. E. Richardson, London 1963

Lowry, Bates, *Renaissance Architecture,* London 1962

Male, Emile, *The Early Churches of Rome*, London 1960
Masson, Georgina, *Italian Villas and Palaces*, London 1959
—— *Italian Gardens*, London 1961
Montigny & Famin, *Architecture Toscane*, 1874
Murray, Peter, *The Architecture of the Italian Renaissance*, London 1969
Pevsner, Nikolaus, *An Outline of European Architecture*, Harmondsworth 1960
Portoghesi, Paolo, *Borromini*, London 1968
Quintavalle, Arturo Carlo, *Il Duomo di Modena*, Firenze 1965
Ricci, Corrado, *Il tempio malatestiano*, Roma 1925
Sanpaolesi, Piero, *La cupola del Brunelleschi*, Firenze 1965
Stokes, Adrian, *Venice, an Aspect of Art*, London 1945
Summerson, Sir John, *The Classical Language of Architecture*, London 1964
Ward-Perkins, J. B., *Constantine and the origin of the Christian Basilica*, PAPERS OF
    THE BRITISH SCHOOL IN ROME 1954
White, John, *Art and Architecture in Italy 1250-1400*, Harmondsworth 1960
Wittkower, Rudolf, *Architectural Principles in the Age of Humanism*, London 1967
—— *Art and Architecture in Italy 1600-1750*, Harmondsworth 1958
Wolfflin, Heinrich, *Renaissance and Baroque*, London 1964

A SHORT GLOSSARY OF TERMS

ambo. In Romanesque architecture elaborate marble pulpits for reading Gospel
    and Epistle
ambulatory. A passage continuing the aisles around the apse of a church
archivolt. The moulded undercurve of an arch
ashlar. Smooth faced rectangular stone used for walling
astylar. A façade without vertical divisions by columns or pilasters
atrium. An open colonnaded quadrangle in front of an Early Christian or
    Romanesque basilica, derived from the open court of the Roman house
attic storey. A low storey above the main cornice of a palace
baldacchino. A canopy on columns over altar or martyr's shrine
bay. Section of nave delimited by columns and transverse arches
chancel. East end of church containing the High Altar, the seats for the clergy
    and the choir
clerestorey. Upper part of nave walls pierced by windows
coffering. Ornamental sunken panels in vault, arch or ceiling
corbel table. Eaves arcading consisting of miniature arches supporting cornice
    on inner or outer wall of a church
crenellation. Battlement with indented parapet
crossing. The area formed by the intersection of nave and transept
diaphragm arch. An arch across the nave supporting a wood ceiling
dosseret. A high stone slab placed on top of a capital to support an arch
drum. A cylindrical or octagonal wall supporting a dome
entablature. The three horizontal sections laid over the capital of a column:
    architrave, frieze and cornice
exedra. An apse-like wall recess or large vaulted niche
finial. A stone ornament on top of a Gothic gable or pinnacle
foil. In Gothic tracery a small arc or lobe between the pointed cusps (trefoil)
iconostasis. A screen with Byzantine icons placed across the nave in front of the
    sanctuary
impost block. A stone slab between the capital of a column and the springing
    of the arch it supports

machicolation. A projecting gallery or parapet in medieval castles and towers with openings at the base for dropping missiles

matroneum. An arcaded gallery round nave and choir reserved for women

mezzanine. A low storey with small windows between the two main lower storeys

narthex. An ante-room inside the basilica, preceding nave and aisles, or an outside portico for the use of new converts (catechumen) and penitents

nymphaeum. A cool, walled-in space with fountains and shaded walks and statues in Roman and Renaissance villas

orders of architecture. Five basic types. *Doric*, sturdy columns with flat (abacus) capital; *Ionic*, with slender column and volute capital; *Corinthian* with acanthus leaf capital; *Composite* and *Tuscan*

ogee arch. A Gothic pointed arch with concave and convex curves

pediment. Triangular gable of low-pitched roof. Also: triangular or segmental head of door or window

pendentive. The triangular concave space ('spherical triangle') between two arches, supporting a cupola

pietra serena. Dark sandstone

presbytery. Eastern part of the church reserved for the clergy

pulvin. In Byzantine architecture a second capital or dosseret to support arch and wall

quoins. Large smooth stones, used at the angles of buildings to strengthen corners

rustication. Great blocks of stone, roughly hewn or worked over, to give strength to external walls at ground floor level of Renaissance palaces

spandrel. Space between two arches in an arcade. Triangle between the sides of an arch and its vertical and horizontal frame

squinch. A small arch (or arches) placed across the interior angles of a square bay to support a dome

stilted arch. An arch whose springing line is not at impost level, but above it, so that its vertical supports are lengthened

string course. A horizontal moulding which projects from the wall surface

trabeation. A straight beam or entablature, immediately above the capitals of columns—in contrast to an arcaded colonnade

transept. The transversal arm of a Latin-Cross church between nave and choir, generally projecting beyond the aisles

tribune. The semicircular or polygonal apse of a basilica

triforium. A dark arcaded passage in the wall of the nave below the clerestorey

tympanum. Triangular or segmental space over a porch, between lintel and arch

vaulting. 1. Tunnel or barrel vault: a continuous semicircular vault, uninterrupted by crossings or intersections. The basic Roman shape of a vault. 2. Groin vault or cross vault: A vault formed by the intersection of two semicircular tunnel vaults of the same dimensions. Groins are the lines of their diagonal intersection. Ribs are the arches alonside the groins, supporting the masonry between them. 3. Gothic rib vaults: a diagonal scheme of multiple ribs supporting pointed arches

voussoir. Wedge-shaped stones composing an arch

window, Serlian (also known as Venetian windows). A window or gateway in three parts, the central one arched and wider than the lateral ones. After Serlio's handbook *L'architettura*, 1551

BIOGRAPHICAL NOTES AND
INDEX TO ARCHITECTS

*A considerable number of notes to architects not mentioned in the text,
have been added to make the list more complete*

Abbondi, Antonio delle (Lo Scarpagnino) (*active* in Venice 1505-49). Milanese. Worked at Palazzo Ducale (Cortile dei Senatori) and at the Fondaco dei Tedeschi (1505-08). Venetian High-Renaissance in the Scuola di S. Rocco façade. The façade is scanned by fluted Corinthian columns on high sockets, dividing it into five bays. Classical tympana on colonettes over the two-part windows, enriched by festoons and consoles, sharply defined entablatures and rich friezes. This ornateness contrasts with the lower storey by Buon, where Coducci's type of semicircular windows and disk patterns and coloured marble prevail. The scuola is famed for Tintoretto's murals.

Alberti, Leon Battista (1404-72). *b.* Genoa, of Florentine descent. Universally gifted Renaissance man. Writer on painting (*Della Pittura* 1436), and *De re aedificatoria* (1452), the ' first architectural treatise of the Renaissance '. Law student in Bologna. In Rome from 1431, employed by the Curia. Theorist and amateur architect. Designed Palazzo Rucellai, Florence, built by Bernardo Rossellino after 1446. For Sigismondo Malatesta of Rimini he designs a Roman exterior for a Gothic church of S. Francis, the Tempio Malatestiano, after 1450. In Florence

he completes S. Maria Novella by a façade in polychrome marble inlay, comparable to S. Miniato. Lastly, S. Sebastiano in Mantua, a centralised church, and S. Andrea, handling Roman motifs more freely. Triumphal arch motif, barrel-vault and aisleless nave

Aleotti, Giovan Battista (Argenta) (1546-1636). Parma. Baroque architect of the dukes Ottavio and Ranuccio Farnese. Built the Teatro Farnese at Parma (1618-28) after the model of Palladio's Teatro Olimpico. Also at Parma the hexagonal church of S. Maria del Quartiere; and at Ferrara the richly decorative façade of the University.

Alessi, Galeazzo (1512-72). Perugia. Formed his style after Michelangelo's in Rome. In his palaces and villas at Genoa where he settled in 1548, he uses a High-Renaissance idiom with two orders of half-columns and pilasters and a recessed central section (Villas Cambiaso, Peschiere, Scassi). Grand courtyards, staircases and colonnades distinguish his palaces, boldly sited on sloping ground. His S. Maria in Carignano, Genoa, is a centrally planned church. In his later works, especially Palazzo Marino, Milan, the exuberant decoration in the cortile d'onore, as in the façade of S. Maria presso S. Celso, the

313

Mannerist trend of subordinating structure to ornament is very marked.

Algardi, Allesandro (1602-54). Bologna. Sculptor and architect, working in Rome since 1625. Baroque classicist. Grassi's façade of S. Ignazio has been erroneously attributed to him; though he executed the stuccoes inside the church. He designed the large villa Pamphili on the Gianicolo, but Grimaldi built it.

Amadeo, Giovanni Antonio (1446-1522). *b.* Pavia. Lombard sculptor and architect. *Active* at the Certosa di Pavia from 1466: sculptural decorations in the cloister and lower half of the façade (1474). His masterpiece is the Colleoni Chapel at Bergamo, adjoining S. Maria Maggiore. After 1500 he works at Milan Cathedral in a belated Gothic style.

Amato, Giacomo (1643 - 1732). Priest-architect, trained in Rome between 1673-85. His masterpiece is the Baroque church of the Pietà in Palermo (1689). Imposing two-tier façade, lofty and narrow with free-standing columns and broken pediment. This and the façade of S. Teresa della Kalsa recall Rinaldi's S. Maria in Campitelli, Rome.

Ammanati, Bartolommeo (1511-92). Mannerist sculptor and architect. With Vignola and Vasari he helped to design Villa Giulia, Rome 1552, and in Florence enlarged Palazzo Pitti and built Ponte S. Trinità (1570).

Angelo da Orvieto (14th century). Umbrian. Between 1322 and 1338 he probably designed the Piazza della Signoria at Gubbio and built its civic palaces, Palazzo dei Consoli and Palazzo del Pretorio, a unified complex carved out of the surrounding hills. The Palace of the Consuls recalls the Captain's Palace at Orvieto. Angelo was active also in Città di Castello, building the Palazzo Comunale, influenced by Palazzo Vecchio in Florence with Gothic two-part windows, crowned by voussoir arches. The massive two-tier block has a high rusticated base with few openings.

Antonio di Vincenzo (14th century). Bologna. *Died* 1401 or 1402. In Bologna he built the Palazzo dei Notai (1381) and the elaborate Palazzo della Mercanzia (begun in 1382). But his greatest work is S. Petronio, a vast north-Italian brick structure, rivalling Milan and Florence cathedrals. Only two bays of the nave were completed by the time of Antonio's death. In scale, lucidity and simplicity the Gothic nave of S. Petronio surpasses its rivals, though the shape of piers and capitals depends from those in Florence Cathedral.

Argenta *see* Aleotti.

Arnolfo di Cambio (*c.* 1245-1302). Florentine sculptor and architect. Assistant of Nicola Pisano. By 1276 established in Rome as independent master. Returns to Florence in 1296. As capomaestro he designs the Cathedral (nave and aisles) and probably also S. Croce (begun in 1295). Arnolfo was influenced by French Gothic architects.

Baccio d'Agnolo (1462-1543). Tuscan. Worked at the gallery of Florentine duomo. Palazzo Bartolino, compact, with corner-quoins in form of pilasters. Flat niches alternate with tabernacle windows. Palazzo Cocchi-Serristori; broad and rusticated basement pilasters; wide arches enframing windows. Roman rather than Tuscan in style.

Bartolomeo da Novara (*active between* 1368-1410). Lombardy. Military architect of Nicolo d'Este of Ferrara for whom he built the brick structure of the Castello d'Estense (begun 1385); and for the Gonzaga at Mantua the Castello di S. Giorgio. (1395).

Battagio, Giovanni (late 15th and early 16th century). Lombardy. Built the centrally planned Renaissance church of the Incoronata at Lodi (1488-1494), in emulation of round temples of Antiquity and early Christian churches like S. Costanza. Architect of Como Cathedral and of S. Maria della Croce, nr. Crema. Dome with octagonal interior. Bramante influence.

Bergamasco *see* Castello.

Bernini, Giovanni Lorenzo (1598-1680). *b*. Naples. Son of Florentine sculptor Pietro Bernini, a Mannerist. In Rome from 1605. Made architect of S. Peter's by Urban VIII in 1629 and henceforth dominates the art of the Roman Baroque as a sculptor, town planner and architect. His first major task is the Baldacchino over the shrine of S. Peter's. He executes the façade of the Palazzo Barberini after Maderno's plan. Builds churches at Castelgandolfo (1658), Ariccia (1662) and his most sophisticated, S. Andrea al Quirinale, Rome 1658-70. Also two Roman palaces Odescalchi and Montecitorio and, for S. Peter's the Scala Regia and the grand colonnade embracing the piazza.

Bianco, Bartolommeo (1590-1657). Como. After 1619 he continues Alessi's tradition of grand palace buildings in Genoa. His Baroque masterpiece is the University and especially its lion-flanked staircase leading to an airy arcaded courtyard with coupled columns. Scenic contrasts between severe, even monotonous façades and resplendent interior courts, constructed on different levels. He built Palazzi Durazzo and Balbi (1620).

Binago, Lorenzo (1554-1628). Milan. Architect of the vast church of S. Alessandro, Milanese version of S. Peter's, Rome. There is a pendentive dome in the centre and to the east a domed extension. By combining two domed areas of different size, the Greek-cross church becomes longitudinal.

Borromini, Francesco (1599-1667). *b*. near Lugano. In Rome since 1617. Assists Maderno then Bernini at Palazzo Barberini and S. Peter's. His Baroque genius for ' setting whole walls into motion ' is unsurpassed. His first church is also his most brilliant, S. Carlo alle Quattro Fontane (1638-46). Oval plan and undulating façade. Then S. Ivo della Sapienza (1642-60). Gives a Baroque interior to S. Giovanni in Laterano (1646-49). Dome, drum and tower of S. Andrea della Fratte. His ripest work is the façade of S. Agnese in Piazza Navona (1653-57). Other works include the Oratory of S. Filippo Neri, the Propaganda Fide and S. Maria dei Sette Dolori (unfinished). In secular architecture he built Palazzo and Villa Falconieri, Rome. Other than Bernini, his great rival, he was a revolutionary and a neurotic. In a fit of maniac depression he took his life.

Boschetto *see* Buschetus.

Bramante, Donato (1444-1514). *b*. near Urbino. Pioneer of the High Renaissance. Grew up in the ambience of Leon Battista Alberti and the artists working at the court of Federico da Montefeltro at the Ducal Palace of Urbino. Fascination with Roman antiquity. Transfers to Milan in 1479 to work for Lodovico Sforza. Influence of Leonardo and of his architectural drawings of round and many-domed churches. In 1482, Bramante rebuilt S. Maria presso S. Satiro and in 1488 worked at Pavia Cathedral. In 1494 follow the polygonal drum and apses of S. Maria delle Grazie; also cloisters of S. Ambrogio, especially the Canon's cloister. In 1499 the French deposed Lodovico, and Bramante left for Rome. He abandons the ornamental Lombard manner and adopts a more severe Roman style, first in the cloister of S. Maria della Pace (1500) and in 1502 when he builds his masterpiece, the Tempietto in S. Pietro in Montorio. On Julius becoming pope in 1502, Bramante was commissioned to replan S. Peter's church and the Vatican. He designs the Belvedere Court, arcades and exedra on a grand scale and evolves his Greek-cross plan and central dome for S. Peter's.

Bramantino (Bartolomeo Suardi) (1465-1536). Lombardy. Painter and architect influenced by Bramante. Worked mainly in Milan for Gian Giacomo Trivulzio. Built the Trivulzio chapel in front of San Nazaro, Milan. It is a family mausoleum, uncommonly severe, in two storeys on a square base. Engaged pilasters are its only decoration. The interior is octagonal.

Briosco, Benedetto (late 15th century). Milanese. Shared with Amadeo work on the façade of the Certosa di Pavia.

Brunelleschi, Filippo (1377-1446). Florence. Creator of the Early Renaissance style in architecture. Started as goldsmith and sculptor. Competed with Ghiberti for first Baptistery door. Visited Rome with Donatello (1402-3). After about 1415 confines himself to architecture. Palazzo di Parte Guelfa. S. Lorenzo (begun 1419) and the Old Sacristy (1421-28). Foundling Hospital (1419-24) and his greatest work, the Dome of Florence Cathedral (1420-36). In S. Croce he built the Pazzi Chapel (1429) and a cloistered forecourt. Second journey to Rome (1433). Designs the first centrally planned church, S. Maria degli Angeli and, in 1436 began S. Spirito, his ripest and most vigorously Roman church. The centre of Palazzo Pitti is attributed to him.

Buon, Giovanni and Bartolomeo, father and son (1355-1443 and 1374-1467). Leading Venetian sculptor-architects of the Early Renaissance. Designed and decorated the Porta della Carta at Palazzo Ducale (1438-42). They had also worked at Ca' d'Oro in the 1420s.

Buontalenti, Bernardo (c. 1536-1608). Florence. Mannerist architect of the Medici dukes. Worked in the Boboli Gardens (Grotta) and built the Medici Villa Pratolino near Florence. After 1574 he continued Vasari's work at the Uffizi, designing the most eccentric doorway since Michelangelo with a pediment broken in two halves, fanning out from the centre. In 1592 he began Palazzo Nonfinito and the year after built the façade of S. Trinità.

Buschetus (Boschetto or Boscheto). Designed Pisa Cathedral, begun in 1063 or 1089 and consecrated in 1118. Buschetus is documented as architect in charge from 1104-10.

Castellamonte, Amadeo di. Turin. d. 1683. He continued the urban modernisation of Turin and built the Palazzo Reale for Carlo Emanuele II of Savoy; also a hunting lodge, the Venaria Reale. He enlarged the town towards the River Po.

Castellamonte, Carlo di (17th century). Turin. Continued the work of Vittozzi as architect in charge of the refashioning of Turin. He unified the streets and created the homogenous Piazza San Carlo (1628).

Castello, Giovan Battista (Il Bergamasco) (1547-1631). Active in Genoa. Richly decorative façade of Palazzo Podestà (1563), overlaid with ornamental stucchi and Mannerist motifs: herms attached to the basement walls, sham wedgestones, frames, and in the *piano nobile*, alternating with tall windows and parapets, a delicate profusion of panoplies, emblems, garlands and stuccoed heads.

Cino, Giuseppe (late 17th, early 18th Century). Lecce. Pupil of Zimbalo. Built Palazzo del Seminario 1694-1709 with florid window-surrounds in the Rococo style between rusticated pilasters on high plinths. A balcony on carved supports over the splendid porch with consoles and figure sculpture is the centre piece. His churches like S. Chiara show the same delicacy of ornamental carvings.

Civitali, Matteo di Giovanni (1436-1501). Lucca. Sculptor and architect, trained in Florence by Rossellino. Works mainly for Lucca Cathedral where he built the beautiful chapel of the Volto Santo, and for other Lucchese churches.

Coducci, Mauro (c. 1440-1504), b. near Bergamo. In Venice from 1469 and, with Pietro Lombardo, her leading Quattrocento architect. Created a distinctive Venetian Renaissance style. 1459: S. Michele in Isola (façade), influenced by Alberti. The lofty façade of S. Zaccaria, the upper storey of the Scuola di S. Marco, the Clock Tower in Piazza S. Marco and the Palazzi Corner-Spinelli and Vendramin-Calergi are among his most notable works. Also the Procuratie Vecchi have been attributed to him. In S. Giovanni Crisostomo he built the first Greek-cross church in Venice.

Cola da Caprarola (early 16th century). Lombardy. *Active* in Umbria where he introduces the centrally planned Greek-cross church of Bramante in the Madonna della Consolazione at Todi (1508) with one semicircular and two polygonal apses, similar to San Biagio at Montepulciano.

Cortona, Pietro Berrettini da (1596-1669). b. Cortona. Leading Baroque painter and architect in Rome. Move to Rome in 1613. Patronised by Cardinal Francesco Barberini. Between 1635 and 1650 he builds SS. Martina e Luca with a two-storey convex façade. In 1656 S. M. della Pace and scenic piazza in front of it. More classical is S. M. in via Lata (1658-62)—barrel vaults, straight trabeation, façade- pediment over triumphal arch are late Roman. Superb dome of S. Carlo al Corso (1668) on groups of clustered pilasters and columns.

Cronaca, (Simone del Pollaiuolo) (1457-1508). Florentine. Trained in Rome. In 1491 completed Palazzo Strozzi (Florence), especially famed for great overhang. Capomaestro of

Florence Cathedral from 1495. Built the Great Hall in Palazzo Vecchio.

His Utopia was an ideal city *Sforzinda* after his patron Francesco Sforza.

Diotisalvi (12th century). Tuscan. He designed the circular domed Baptistery in Pisa (begun 1153-54). His name is inscribed on the main portal. The shape of the cupola was altered in the Gothic style, probably by Nicola Pisano, around 1278.

Dotti, Carlo Francesco (1670-1759). Bologna. Late Baroque architect. His masterpiece is the large hill-sanctuary, the Madonna di S. Luca, near Bologna (1723-57.) It is a domed elliptical church with undulating out-buildings in front and attached sanctuary at the rear. The Greek-cross plan is circumscribed by an oval. Externally the sanctuary is a complex of geometrical bodies, preceded by a pedimented triumphal arch, projecting from the wings, which terminate in polygonal pavilions—a spectacular prelude to the lofty drum and dome.

Fanzago, Cosimo (1591 - 1678). Bergamo. Became the leading architect of the full Baroque in Naples. His cloisters in the Certosa di S. Martino are of restrained elegance; but the church interior, as that of Montecassino attributed to him, has a polychrome richness of decoration. Like Bernini he was an all rounder—architect, sculptor, painter. His masterpiece is the domed Greek-cross church of S. Maria Egiziaca. Other works like S. Giuseppe degli Scalzi (façade) or the Guglia di S. Gennaro excel by profuse, sometimes incongruous decoration.

Filarete, Antonio (1400 - 69). Author of *Trattato d'Architettura* and architect of the vast Ospedale Maggiore in Milan, dependent from Brunelleschi's Foundling Hospital.

Fontana, Carlo (1634-1714). *b.* Como. In Rome from about 1655. The leading architect of Late Baroque Classicism in Rome and for ten years Bernini's chief assistant. He completed Pelazzo Montecitorio, altering Bernini's design. His most characteristic work is the façade of S. Marcello al Corso (1682). The concave façade is sculpturally defined by projecting orders and entablatures. Double columns on square plinths frame the central bay; pilasters in the upper tier. Here palm branches serve as volutes and an aedicule crowns a broken pediment. Though the elements are baroque, the façade is calm and ' static '. Fontana's activity was prolific and he built many chapels in the churches of Rome (Cappella Cibo in S. Maria del Popolo; Cappella Ginetti in S. Andrea della Valle; Baptismal chapel in S. Peter's). He also took a hand in town planning and was twice president of the Accademia di S. Luca.

Fontana, Domenico (1543-1607). *b.* Lugano. Went to Rome in 1563. Rebuilt the Lateran Palace for Pope Sixtus V, a severe and powerful though monotonous structure; also the Scala Santa. Villa Montalto for the same pope with waterworks, fountains, gardens. Fontana heralds the Baroque, especially in town planning. He installed the Acqua Felice to supply the fountains of Rome. His scheme for a network of streets, radiating from S. Maria Maggiore in five directions was accomplished between 1585 and 1590. His master plan for the city was called *piano regolatore*. In S. Maria Maggiore he built the monumental Cappella Sistina, a sober cinquecento structure, but in sumptuous polychrome marble to which Ponzio's Cappella Paolina (1611) formed the counterpart.

Formigine, Andrea da Marchesi (active first half of 16th century). Bologna. Built High-Renaissance palaces with marked Mannerist features, all in Bologna. Palazzo Fantuzzi (1517), smooth walling, but strange rustication on paired columns, door and window jambs and consoles. Search for new decorative motifs. In Palazzo Castagnoli (1528) contrasting materials in stone portico and brick upper storey. Engaged columns below continued in slender shafts. Semicircular pediments echo the arches of the loggia. Palazzo Salina Amorini (1525) with typical Bolognese portico. Bead moulding on arches; flat window pilasters; roundels with sculptured heads in pendentives. Palazzo Malvezzi Campeggi, designed by Formigine built by his son c. 1550. Decorations restricted to abstract reliefs: roundels on end pilasters, disks between arches and lace-like arabesques of friezes. The fine courtyard recalls Palazzo Bevilacque. Semicircular arcade topped by loggias whose shafts are centred alternately over the columns and the apex of arches.

Francesco di Giorgio (1439-1502). b. Siena. Protagonist of the Early Renaissance. Universally gifted sculptor, painter, architect and military engineer. Employed by Federico da Montefeltro at the Palace of Urbino (after 1472). Castles of S. Leo and Sassocorvaro. Probably designed S. Bernardino, Urbino; the Ducal Palace at Jesi and, his finest church, S. Maria del Calcinaio, near Cortona (1485), combining a Latin-cross plan with centralised sanctuary and dome.

Fuga, Ferdinando (1699-1782). b. Florence, d. Naples. Late Baroque architect whose best work was done in Rome between 1730 and 1750. Palazzo della Consulta (1732-37) with an immensely varied façade; two tiers, three portals, where figures recline on pediments as Michelangelo's on the sarcophagi of the Medici Chapel. Tabernacle windows framed by half pilasters. Other motifs are rusticated supports and mezzanine in the basement, roof balusters, light and dark panels alternating. The Consulta façade is as elegant and sophisticated as Palazzo Corsini (1736) is austere. Small church of S. Maria della Morte: baroque façade, but staid and regular; oval interior and cupola. His Late Baroque classicism is also apparent in the façade of S. Maria Maggiore (1741-43), the well defined orders and entablatures and crowning pediments over large dark openings. Palazzo Bolognetti (1745) follows the scheme of 16th century palaces in its classical purity and regularity, and pilasters alternating with windows. In 1751 Fuga left Rome for Naples, where he built the broad planar façade of the Gerolamini church, flanked by bell towers recalling those of S. Agnese in Piazza Navona.

Galilei, Alessandro (1691-1737). Florentine. Architect of the classicising façade of S. Giovanni in Laterano and that of S. Giovanni dei Fiorentini, Rome.

Gattapone, Matteo (14th century). Umbrian. Built the Rocca di Spoleto for Cardinal Albernoz, c. 1362-70. This hill fortress consists of two walled rectangles of different height with six end-towers. In Bologna Matteo built the Collegio di Spagna for the same patron with a double arcade on polygonal columns.

Giocondo, Fra (1435-1515). *b.* Verona. Appointed by Leo X to assist Raphael with the rebuilding of S. Peter's.

Giotto di Bondone (1266-1337). Florentine painter and, in his last years, appointed capomaestro of the Cathedral in Florence (1334-37). Designed its Campanile: Giotto's Tower.

Giulio Romano (1499-1546). *b.* Rome. Painter and architect. Raphael's pupil and assistant in the Loggias and Stanze del Vaticano. Helped to decorate Villa Madama. In 1524 became court-architect of Federico Gonzaga of Mantua. Protagonist of the Mannerist style. Palazzo del Tè (1526-31) long one-storey façade, and colonnaded portico on the garden side. Massive rustication and wilfully used Roman motifs. Eccentricities like dislodged keystones etc. More restrained in his own house (1544). Also worked in the Ducal Palace and reconstructed Mantua Cathedral.

Grassi, Orazio (1583-1654). Rome. Jesuit father and architect of S. Ignazio, the largest church in Rome. (1626-50). The design of the façade resembles that of della Porta's Il Gesù. Massive volutes and a heavy attic fuse the two halves; closely set pilasters stress the vertical of the imposing façade which dwarfs the intimate Piazza with its small curving house fronts ' spreading like wings on a stage '. (Wittkower).

Grigi, Guglielmo (*active* in Venice 1515-30). Bergamo. Completed the Procuratie Vecchie (started by Coducci). Two-tier loggias above the fifty arcades of the covered portico opposite the Procuratie Nuove, forming the trapezoid Piazza S. Marco.

Guarini, Guarino (1624-83). *b.* Modena. Member of the Theatine Order. Mathematical bend. Follower of Borromini in his preference for oval plan and undulating outer walls. Palazzo Carignano, Turin (1679). His outstanding Baroque creations are all in Turin: the Chapel of S. Sindone and the Church of S. Lorenzo. Eccentric domes and spires. Sophisticated geometry. He wrote on *Architettura civile*.

Juvarra, Filippo (1678-1736). *b.* Messina. Greatest Rococo architect in Italy. Pupil of Carlo Fontana in Rome. Since 1714 active at the Court of King Victor Amadeus of Savoy. Urban planning in Turin. Chief works: the spectacular sanctuary of La Superga (Turin) and the Royal Hunting Lodge of Stupinigi (1719). Star-like radiation of wings. Palazzo Madama and other royal palaces, villas and churches. In the sheer volume of creative work and his Rococo brilliance Juvarra is comparable to Tiepolo.

Laurana, Luciano (*c.* 1420-79). *b.* Dalmatia. *Active* at the Montefeltro court at Urbino between 1468 and 1472, redesigning the Ducal Palace. Immaculate Quattrocento style of the Grand Courtyard, interior architecture and decoration, continued after his departure by Francesco di Giorgio and a host of craftsmen from Florence and northern Italy.

Leoni, Leone (1509-90). Arezzo. Sculptor and architect. *Active* mainly in Lombardy. In 1573 he built for himself Palazzo Omenoni (Milan) with herm sculptures of bearded captives attached to the pilasters and supporting the cornice. (Pl. 181, in my *Italian Sculpture*.) Left Italy for Spain to work for Charles V.

Ligorio, Pirro (1500-83). *b.* Naples. Mannerist architect. The monumental Villa d'Este at Tivoli (1550) with its waterworks and symmetrical terraced gardens is his principal claim to fame. The more intimate Villa Pia for Pope Pius IV (1562) is of classical inspiration. Ligorio was a learned antiquarian and archaeologist.

Lombardo, Pietro (*c.* 1435-1515). *b.* Carona (Lombardy). Together with Mauro Coducci, the leading Venetian architect (and sculptor) during the later Quattrocento. Active at Venice since 1467. His outstanding work is S. Maria dei Miracoli (1481-89), a synthesis of Venetian marble panelling, Byzantine dome and Renaissance mouldings. The lower half of the Scuola di S. Marco façade is also his. Geometrical interrelation of semicircle and rectangle.

Longhena, Baldassare (1598-1682). *b.* Venice. Leading Venetian Baroque architect. Pupil of Scamozzi. His life's work is S. Maria della Salute (1630-82) with its landmark cupola and voluted buttresses, commanding the entrance to the Canale Grande. Radiating vistas from the entrance into the octagonal interior. Longhena designed, but did not complete, Palazzo Pesaro and Palazzo Rezzonico, taking Sansovino's Palazzo Corner Ca' Grande as his model.

Longhi, Martino, the Younger (1602-60). High Baroque architect, active in Rome. Opposite Fontana Trevi he built SS. Vincenzo ed Anastasio (1646-50), his ripest work, with free-standing triple columns flanking the centre of both storeys. Pomp and power of the full Baroque combine with Mannerist features. He also completed S. Carlo al Corso in Rome.

Lurago, Rocco. Genoese architect of palaces alongside the deeply sloping Strada Nuova. In Palazzo Doria-Tursi (1564) he introduces a sequence of vistas from the entrance hall through the inner court to the staircase behind. It becomes the prototype of palace architecture in Genoa.

Maderno, Carlo (1556-1629). *b.* near Lugano. Architect of the early Baroque in Rome. Since 1588 assistant of his uncle Domenico Fontana in Rome. His first and finest independent work is the façade of S. Susanna. In 1603 became architect in charge of S. Peter's where he added the nave to Michelangelo's centralised plan and built the imposing but too extended façade (1607-12). His cupola of S. Andrea della Valle is second only to Michelangelo's. Maderno built Palazzo Mattei and designed and began Palazzo Barberini (1629) which Bernini altered and completed.

Magenta, Giovanni (1565-1635). Bologna. General of the Barnabite Order. Designed the vast Cathedral of S. Pietro, Bologna (1599) and also S. Salvatore (1605), a monumental hall church with free-standing columns in the nave, separated from the domed crossing. By its massiveness it is Early Baroque. In S. Paolo (1611) he created a variation on the theme of Il Gesù.

Maiano, Benedetto da (1442-97). Florentine sculptor and architect. Built Palazzo Strozzi after the model of Michelozzo's Palazzo Medici. Palazzo Strozzi is rusticated throughout; it was begun in 1489 and completed by Cronaca who added the huge overhanging cornice.

Maiano, Giuliano da (1432-90). Tuscan architect of the Early Renaissance in the following of Alberti, Brunelleschi, Michelozzo. Collaborates with his brother, the sculptor Benedetto da Maiano. His finest work is Palazzo Spannocchi at Siena, nobly proportioned, rusticated throughout, with slender two-part windows and no vertical divisions by pilasters. Delicately moulded string courses divide the three storeys. Fully sculptured heads are inserted between the shapely consoles carrying the roof cornice. In 1474 Giuliano began to build the Cathedral of Faenza, a three-aisled basilica in the style of Brunelleschi. He also worked at Naples (Porta Capuana) and at the pilgrimage church of Loreto.

Mangone, Fabio (1587-1629). Milan. Cathedral architect from 1617 to 1629. Together with Ricchino he executed the portals of Milan Cathedral. Cardinal Federico Borromini commissioned the Ambrosiana Library from him. Severely classical style in the Cortile of the Collegio Elvetico with its two tier rows of Doric and Ionic columns and straight trabeation.

Mantegazza, Cristoforo (d. 1482) and **Antonio** (d. 1495). Sculptor-architects who shared with Amadeo the construction of the Certosa di Pavia façade and its decorative reliefs and statuettes.

Marchionni, Carlo (1702-86). Rome. Architect of the Villa Albani (1746-63) to house the Cardinal's art collection, assembled by Winckelmann. Vast two-tier casino with Palladian portico, nine arches, separated by banded pilasters. In the upper storey ornate window surrounds roof balusters and statues. The crescent shaped Caféhaus encircling the garden is a one storey arcade, also with roof balusters and statues. Transition from Rococo to Neo-Classicism.

Masegne, dalle, Pierpaolo (d. 1403) and **Jacobello** (d. 1409). Venice. Gothic sculptors and architects, employed in S. Mark's Cathedral (Iconostasis) and Palazzo Ducale (central balcony and window of façade facing the lagoon, 1404). In 1399 they worked at the fabric of Milan Cathedral and also at the Visconti Castle at Pavia.

Massari, Giorgio (c. 1686-1766). Venice. Architect of the transition from Rococo to Neo-Classicism. His chief works are the churches of the Gesuati (1725-36) and of the Visitation (1745-60); also Palazzo Grassi-Stucky (1705-45). The Palladian temple façade of Gesuati on the Giudecca has a giant order of columns, large statues and a classical entablature and pediment. The aisleless interior has side chapels with altarpieces by Tiepolo, Piazzetta and Ricci and a spacious sanctuary behind the altar. The three ceiling-frescoes by Tiepolo, glorifying the life of S. Dominic, add great splendour to the interior architecture. The church of the Visitation or della Pietà has an oval plan and vaulted ceiling, also decorated by Tiepolo. The elliptical nave combines with a planar presbytery. Palazzo Grassi is the most monumental 18th century palace in Venice; classicising in its calm symmetery, the arched first floor windows and Corinthian pilasters, the smooth rustication of the basement and the tripartite portal at the water's edge.

Michelangelo Buonarotti (1475-1564). Florentine. Sculptor, painter, architect of the High Renaissance whose work contains the roots of Mannerism as well as Baroque. His first architectural commission came in 1520, the Medici Chapel in San Lorenzo, Florence and in 1524 the Laurentian Library and Vestibule. Use of supporting elements for ornamental purposes. Settles in Rome for good in 1534. Redesigning of the Capitol begins in 1539. Completes the façade and upper storeys of the courtyard in Palazzo Farnese (1546). The last eighteen years of his life Michelangelo devoted to the rebuilding of S. Peter's, modifying Bramante's centralised plan.

Michelozzo, Michelozzi (1396-1472). Florentine. Started in Ghiberti's workshop. Built Dominican monastery of S. Marco (1437-52) in Florence. Between 1425 and 1433 shared work and workshop with Donatello. Becomes chief architect of Florence Cathedral after Brunelleschi's death in 1446. Favoured architect of the Medici. Built their family palace Medici-Riccardi and inner court (1444-59) and modernised their villas at Careggi (1433) and Fiesole (1458). In the church of the Annunziata he designed the centrally planned tribune. Since 1462 active in Milan, where he built the Portinari Chapel in S. Eustorgio.

Morandi, Antonio (Terribilia) (d. 1568). Bologna. Late Renaissance architect. In 1562 he built the Archiginnasio an immensely long one-storey building with a covered portico of thirty arches. The sequence of arches corresponds with the fine aedicule windows above, each crowned by an elegant emblematical stone carving.

Orcagna, Andrea di Cione (active 1343-1368). Florence. Painter, sculptor and architect of the late Gothic. Capomaestro of Or San Michele in

1356 for which he made the architectural tabernacle (1359). Supervising architect of Orvieto Cathedral (1358-62). One of the façade mosaics is by him. In 1366 he became consultant to Florence Cathedral, helping to evolve its final plan.

Palladio, Andrea (1508-80). b. Padua. In 1524 enters Stonemason's Guild at Vicenza. Educated in Roman art and letters by his Vicentine patron Giangiorgio Trissino. Profound interest in archaeology and Roman architecture which determine his style and his theory. *Quattro Libri dell'Architettura*, published in 1570. Powerful High Renaissance style in the palaces of Vicenza and his two churches in Venice. Mathematical and symmetrical planning also in his villas. In Vicenza his Basilica (1549), Palazzo Chiericati (1556) and Loggia del Capitano (1571) and the massive palaces Thiene, Valmarana, Porto etc. determine the Roman aspect of the city. His country villas, based on square or circle, preceded by a portico, blend with the landscape. Most famous La Rotonda (c. 1550), La Malcontenta (1560) and Villa Maser (1560s). S. Giorgio Maggiore (1566) and Il Redentore (1576) are domed basilicas with classical temple-fronts; both in Venice. He also designed the façade of S. Francesco della Vigna (1562).

Penna, Cesare. Lecce. Built the upper tier of S. Croce (1644) in the most sumptuously Baroque ornamental style overlaying the firm structural forms (*see* note on Gabriele Riccardi).

Peruzzi, Baldassare (1481-1536). b. Siena. Perhaps the most brilliant architect of the High Renaissance in Rome, follower of Bramante and

323

Raphael. 1508-11 built Villa Farnesina for Agostino Chigi, decorated by Raphael, Giulio Romano and himself. Architect in charge of S. Peter's after Raphael's death in 1520. With Antonio da Sangallo he began the pentagonal Villa Farnese at Caprarola which Vignola completed. His most original work in Rome is Palazzo Massimi alle Colonne with curving façade and Roman portico and sumptuous inner courtyard, a Mannerist ensemble of great distinction.

Piranesi, Giovanni Battista (1720-78). Venice. In Rome from 1745. Etcher of Roman ruins and fantasies. Built the church of S. Maria del Priorato in a Neo-Classical, yet decorative style. Also the Villa of the Cavalieri di Malta with a fanciful entrance, made up of Roman trophies and armoury: a baroque interpretation of classical motifs, with an archaeological flavour.

Ponzio, Flaminio (1560-1613). Lugano. Active in Rome from 1591. Patronised by Borghese Pope Paul V. Designed Cappella Paolina in S. Maria Maggiore as a counterpart to the Chapel of Pope Sixtus V. Together they form a transept to the Basilica. Late Renaissance style, imposing and sumptuous in multi-coloured marble. Mannerist overloading with niche sculptures, reliefs, heavy entablatures and triumphal arch motifs. In 1605 he began the enlargement of the Quirinal Palace, completed by Maderna, and in 1612 the Acqua Paola, a monumental wall-fountain, with five arched recesses from which the water cascades into a basin. With his assistant Vasanzio he reconstructed S. Sebastiano fuori le Mura in a style of classical sobriety.

Porta, Giacomo della (1537-1602). b. Lombardy. Worked mainly in Rome. He completed Michelangelo's palaces on the Capitol and in 1573 became chief architect of S. Peter's, changing the shape of Michelangelo's dome and building the smaller cupolas. He modified Vignola's epoch-making façade of Il Gesù and completed most of the interior. 1582-92 Nave of S. Giovanni dei Fiorentini. His last work was the spectacular Villa Aldobrandini at Frascati.

Preti, Francesco Maria (1701-84). Castelfranco. Architect of the Villa Pisani at Strà, the most stately villa on the Brenta, classicising in Palladio's manner. A projecting centrepiece with eight engaged columns on a high rusticated base is crowned by a frieze, pediment and statues and flanked by two long wings with pilaster divisions. The villa, built for Doge Alvise Pisani between 1735-56, has Tiepolo's ceiling painting 'The Glorification of the Pisani family' in the Grand Salone.

Raguzzini, Filippo (1680-1771). Rome. Architect and town planner of the Rococo. Piazza S. Ignazio (1727-28). Striking contrast between elegant curving frontages of small houses facing the imposing façade of S. Ignazio. Enclosed oval space and near view of church.

Rainaldi, Carlo (1611-91). b. Rome. High Baroque architect. He started S. Agnese in Piazza Navona, but was replaced by Borromini. He is best known by the twin churches in Piazza del Popolo: S. Maria dei Miracoli and S. Maria in Monte Santo which Bernini completed. He also designed the over decorated façade of S. Andrea della Valle and built S.

Maria in Campitelli (1663-67) in the Roman grand manner.

Rainaldus. Began the nave extension of Pisa Cathedral (three bays to the west) and also the façade (completed in the 1180s).

Raphael (Raffaello Sanzio) (1483-1520). *b.* Urbino. Painter and architect of the High Renaissance. In Rome from 1508. Friend of Bramante whose classical style is reflected in his paintings: round temple in the *Betrothal of the Virgin* in the Brera, and coffered vaults in the *School of Athens*. He built a domed and centralised church in Rome, S. Eligio degli Orefici, and Palazzo Vidoni-Caffarelli. As surveyor of Roman Antiquities under Pope Leo X, he became closely acquainted with the buildings of Imperial Rome which influenced his style in Villa Madama (1516) with its vaulting, niches and luxuriant decorations. He was also co-architect of S. Peter's, changing Bramante's central into a basilican plan. His last building was the Chigi Chapel in S. Maria del Popolo.

Riccardi, Gabriele. Lecce. Before 1582 he began S. Croce, the finest church in Lecce, completed in 1644 by Cesare Penna who built the profusely decorated upper tier. Fusion of the Apulian Romanesque with a wealth of ornamental relief and figure sculpture. Animal caryatides support a long row of balusters across the façade; rich friezes, oculi windows engaged columns, six in the lower, four in the upper tier scan the imposing façade.

Ricchino, Francesco Maria (1583-1658). Milan. Leading Lombard architect of the Early Baroque, rejecting Mannerism. Sent to Rome by Cardinal Federico Borromeo. From 1631-38 he is architect in charge of Milan Cathedral. His early masterpiece is S. Giuseppe, Milan (1607-16). A large Greek-cross nave with a dome on four lofty arches is joined to a small east end. The façade derives from Maderno's S. Susanna, Rome and is independent from the interior, but attached to the domed octagon. There are two superimposed central sections with pediments, the upper one buttressed by volutes in the baroque fashion. Ricchino designed the vast courtyard of the Ospedale Maggiore, Milan. In 1627 he built the first concave façade of the Baroque (Collegio Elvetico), a shallow semicircle with quoins at the ends and a convex baluster over the portal. For the Palazzo di Brera he created the noble cortile with two storeys of well spaced arcades on paired columns and elegant balusters.

Rizzo, Antonio (*active c.* 1465-1500). Verona. Sculptor-architect. Protomagister of Palazzo Ducale, Venice, after the fire of 1483. Introduces the Renaissance style into the Gothic building. His masterpiece is the Scala dei Giganti and the loggias of the Cortile in the east wing of the palace. Profusion of precious marble inlays and Victory reliefs. In 1498 he fled from Venice on charges of embezzlement.

Rossellino, Bernardo (1409-64). *b.* Settignano near Florence. Sculptor and architect. Acting hand of Leon Battista Alberti. He built Palazzo Rucellai in Florence after Alberti's design (1446-51) and the Cortile after his own. Pope Pius II commissioned him to build the Cathedral, bishop's palace and Palazzo Piccolomini at Pienza; the former influenced by Alberti's Tempio Malatestiano in Rimini, the latter by Palazzo Rucellai. But the three-tier garden loggias are wholly original. The two palaces converging towards the Cathedral are a fine example of Renaissance town planning.

Rossetti, Biagio (1465-1516). Bologna. *Active* mainly in Ferrara where he began Palazzo Diamanti, characteristic for its diamond-shaped blocks covering both storeys. The noble simplicity of a classical palace surpasses its model, the late medieval Palazzo Bevilacqua in Bologna, which introduced this type of rustication. Palazzo Diamanti was completed in 1565. Biagio served Ercole I as town architect and also built Palazzo Costabile.

Rossi, Giovan Antonio de' (1616-95). Rome. Late Baroque architect. S. Maria in Campo Marzo. Palazzo Altieri in the Piazza del Gesù—his largest work (1650-54)—enlarged by two wings under the Altieri Pope Clement X. Austere front: three tiers with central balcony over portal; rusticated corner pilasters. Traditional, with few Baroque characteristics. More original is Palazzo Bonaparte, free-standing with rounded corners, elegant curved window pediments and Borrominesque decorations, a prelude to the Rococo.

Salvi, Nicola (1697-1751). Rome. Fontana Trevi, a sculptural and architectural monument of the full Baroque, a stage set of palace façade, Corinthian columns and triumphal arch with Neptune ensconced on a shell and, in front of him, a huge basin with natural rocks and waterfalls, tritons and seahorses in dynamic movement.

Sanctis, Francesco de (1693-1740). Architect of the shapely Rococo stairway, the ' Spanish Steps ' in Rome; leading in elegant curves from Piazza di Spagna up to the Trinità dei Monti.

Sanfelice, Ferdinando (1675-1750). Naples. Rococo architect of great productivity, imagination and elegance. Chiesa delle Nunziatelle (Naples); multicoloured façade and nave; high vault, decorated by de Mura's *Assumption*. Long frontage of Palazzo Serra Cassano. Sanfelice excels in monumental staircases of great daring and Borrominesque convexities as in Palazzo Bartolomeo di Majo.

Sangallo, Antonio da, the younger (1485-1546). *b.* Florence. Eminent High Renaissance architect in Rome, follower of Bramante, Raphael, Peruzzi. Assists in the work at S. Peter's. His greatest building is Palazzo Farnese, Rome (1534-46), completed by Michelangelo. Since 1536 architect in charge of S. Peter's. His style was classical, grave, Roman, unaffected by Mannerism.

Sangallo, Antonio da, the elder (1455-1534). Florentine architect and military engineer. His one outstanding work is the domed, Greek-cross church of S. Biagio at Montepulciano (1519-28), a realisation of Bramante's first plan for S. Peter's. Only one of the four projected towers is completed.

Sangallo, Giuliano da (1445-1516). Architect, sculptor, engineer. Belated follower of Brunelleschi, especially in the Greek-cross church of S. Maria delle Carceri (Prato) 1485, the first of its kind in the Renaissance with marble exterior and ' Brunelleschian interior '. For Lorenzo Medici he converted Villa Poggio a Caiano and in Florence he built Palazzo Gondi, close in style to Michelozzo's Medici palace.

Sanmicheli, Michele (1485-1559). *b.* Verona. With Sansovino and

Palladio the greatest architect of the Veneto. Went to Rome in 1500 for training. Worked on fortifications in the papal states; then in Verona (since 1527) and for Venice. Porta Pallio and Porta Nuova, both at Verona; strong rusticated gateways with Doric columns. In palace architecture he derives from Bramante and Raphael; he is attracted by late Roman architecture and develops a richly ornamental and sculptural style with Mannerist variations of the classical orders, pediments and arches. Palazzo Pompei, Canossa, Bevilacqua, all in Verona between 1530-37, and later in Venice, Palazzo Grimani. (*c.* 1556.)

Sansovino, Jacopo (1486-1570). *b.* Florence. Sculptor-architect who brought the High Renaissance style to Venice. Pupil of Andrea Sansovino whose name he adopted. In Rome from 1505-27. Then settled in Venice for life. Becomes proto-magister of S. Mark's in 1529. Determined the new cityscape of Venice by his buildings designed to harmonize with the Doge's Palace: the Library and Mint (1537-54) and the Loggetta beneath the Campanile which he also decorated with sculpture. His greatest palace in the Roman style is Palazzo Corner di Ca' Grande (*c.* 1560). Among his Venetian churches is S. Francesco della Vigna; façade by Palladio.

Sardi, Giuseppe (*c.* 1630-99). Lugano. *Active* in Venice after 1663. Late Baroque architect, follower of Scamozzi and Longhena. Façades of S. Salvatore (1663), S. Maria del Giglio (1680-83), Church of the Scalzi (1683-89). S. Maria del Giglio, beside S. Moisé, has the most lavishly decorated façade of the Venetian Rococo. Niche sculptures between paired columns, whose plinths are overlaid with reliefs, glorify the House of Barbaro. There are figures in movement even on the broken pediment of the two-tier church. The Scalzi façade on the Canale Grande is more staid and balanced. Its two storeys are syncopated by twin columns framing niches. The plinths have circular patterns and there are free-standing sculptures on top of the pediment.

Scalfarotto, Giovanni Antonio (1700-64). Venice. Architect of S. Simeone and Giudea (1718-38), the picturesque landmark opposite the station. It is a Venetian synthesis of Byzantine dome and Palladian temple front as well as a copy of the Roman Pantheon. A steep flight of stairs leads from the Grand Canal to a classical atrium on four Corinthian columns, attached to the cylindrical body of the church with semicircular apses. The dome is of unusual height in relation to the dimensions of S. Simeone.

Scamozzi, Vincenzo (1552-1616). *b.* Vicenza. Venetian Mannerist and imitator of Palladio. His masterpiece is Villa Pisani at Lonigo. He completed S. Giorgio Maggiore in Venice and designed the backdrops for the Teatro Olimpico at Vicenza, both by Palladio. In 1586 he started building the Procuratie Nuove, completed by Longhena in 1640. After journeying to Rome and Naples he wrote his *Discorsi sopra le antichita di Roma* (1582) and at the end of his life *L'idea dell'architettura universale* (1615). His work is eclectic and academic such as the Palladian theatre at Sabionetta.

Scarpagnino, *see* Abbondi

Solari, Guiniforte (1429-81). Milan. Belated Gothicist. He contributed

327

Rome since 1530. Leading exponent of the Mannerist style. In 1550 he completed the pentagonal Villa Farnese at Caprarola including the circular courtyard and the garden. Between 1550-55 he collaborated with Vasari and della Porta at the Villa Giulia with its Nymphaeum and semicircular courtyard and architectural gardens. His epoch making work was the church of Il Gesù, Rome, begun in 1568, combining a domed centre with an aisle-less longitudinal nave and many chapels. Master in charge of S. Peter's from 1567-73.

Vittone, Bernardo (*c.* 1704-70). Piemontese. Heir to Juvarra and Guarini. Rococo architect of provincial sanctuaries and centralised churches. Vallinotto, near Carignano (1738-90) has a plain white dome diminishing in tiers; S. Chiara at Brà (1742) a domical vault with windows revealing a painted sky inside the 'diaphanous' shell. S. Maria di Piazza (Turin), 1751-1754 introduces concave pendentives fusing with the drum. S. Croce at Villanova di Mondovi also aims at interior unification of pendentives, drum and dome.

Vittozzi, Ascanio (1539 - 1615). Orvieto. Assistant of Domenico Fontana in Rome. Called to Turin by Duke Carlo Emmanuele to modernize the medieval city. He built the via Roma and refashioned the façades alongside it. He also built churches, S. Spirito, SS. Trinità, Corpus Domini.

Zaccagni, Bernardino (1455-1530). Emilia. Architect of the centrally planned Greek-cross church of the Madonna della Steccata, Parma, with small octagonal chapels around the perimeter, four apses at the end of each arm and an imposing dome.

Zimbalo, Giuseppe (2nd half of 17th century). Lecce (Apulia). Refashioned the cathedral of Lecce (1659-82) in the sumptuous and scenographic style of the full Baroque. Richly carved church façades, S. Agostino, Chiesa del Rosario.

Zingarello *see* Zimbalo.

INDEX TO BUILDINGS

(The figures refer to illustrations)

332

ITALIAN REGIONS AND THEIR PROVINCES

1. LIGURIA.
   Genova, Imperia, La Spezia, Savona
2. PIEDMONT.
   Alessandria, Aosta, Asti, Cuneo, Novara, Turin, Vercelli
3. LOMBARDY.
   Bergamo, Brescia, Como, Cremona, Mantova, Milano, Pavia,
   Sondrio, Varese
4. VENETIA.
   Belluno, Friuli, Padua, Rovigo, Treviso, Venice, Verona, Vicenza,
   Carnaro, Gorizia, Istria, Trieste, Zara, Bolzano, Trento
5. EMILIA.
   Bologna, Ferrara, Forlì, Modena, Parma, Piacenza, Ravenna,
   Reggio Emilia
6. TUSCANY.
   Apuania, Arezzo, Firenze, Grosseto, Leghorn, Lucca, Pisa,
   Pistoia, Siena
7. MARCHES.
   Ancona, Ascoli Piceno, Macerata, Pesaro/Urbino
8. UMBRIA.
   Perugia, Terni
9. ABRUZZI/MOLISE.
   Aquila, Campobasso, Chieti, Pescara, Teramo
10. LAZIO (Latium).
    Frisinone, Littoria, Rieti, Rome, Viterbo
11. CAMPANIA.
    Avellino, Benevento, Napoli, Salerno
12. AFULIA.
    Bari, Brindisi, Foggia, Lecce, Taranto (Ionio)
13. LUCANIA.
    Matera, Potenza
14. CALABRIA.
    Catanzaro, Cosenza, Reggio Calabria
15. SICILY.   Siracusa, Trapani
    Agrigento, Caltanissetta, Catania, Enna, Messina, Palermo, Ragusa,
16. SARDINIA.
    Cagliari, Nuoro, Sassari

GENERAL INDEX

(The bold figures refer to the illustrations)